Lord Increase Our Faith

LORD Increase Our Faith

NEAL A. MAXWELL

BOOKCRAFT
SALT LAKE CITY, UTAH

Library of Congress Catalog Card Number: 94-70144
ISBN 0-88494-919-2

Second Printing, 1994

Printed in the United States of America

To him that overcometh will I grant to sit with me in my throne, even as I also overcame, and am set down with my Father in his throne.

—*Revelation 3:21*

They are they who received the testimony of Jesus . . . and who overcome by faith. . . . These shall dwell in the presence of God and his Christ forever and ever.

—*D&C 76:51, 53, 62*

Contents

Acknowledgments

The portions of July available to do this writing would not have been adequate without several quick "turn arounds" of drafts made possible by ever-thoughtful and able Susan Jackson, aided briefly by Sandra Thueson. Somehow, Susan got everything else done as well.

Whatever this book's deficiencies, they would have been more numerous without the help of the following individuals: Readers H. E. "Bud" Scruggs and Liz Haglund made valuable and candid suggestions. Chapter 4 was reviewed and enriched by Royal Skousen, Jack Welch, and Richard Turley. For chapter 6 Dr. John C. Nelson supplied useful suggestions on the balance of the physical body and the individual spirit.

At Bookcraft, Cory Maxwell gave early commentary and refining observations. Being blessed with only one son, I am glad that son is Cory. George Bickerstaff was especially helpful with his usual and careful editing of the manuscript for publication.

Colleen, as always, encouraged, but did so while urging me not to push too hard in July.

This is not an official Church publication. The author alone is responsible for the content and its limitations.

Introduction

"Lord, increase our faith" (Luke 17:5).

It is significant that this poignant apostolic request came from the Twelve *after* they had already seen Jesus heal Peter's mother-in-law, a leper, a paralytic, a withered hand, and the centurion's servant. They had observed Him cast out devils; raise from the dead a widow's son and Jairus's daughter; still the tempest; cast out a legion of devils; feed the five thousand; and be transfigured on the Mount. Yet they still asked!

Clearly, if seeing such multiple miracles had produced sustained faith, the apostolic plea would never have been made.

In his poem "Dover Beach," Matthew Arnold, made this eloquent observation about faith in his time.

> The sea of faith
> Was once, too, at the full, and round earth's shore
> Lay like the folds of a bright girdle furled;
> But now I only hear
> Its melancholy, long, withdrawing roar,
> Retreating, to the breath
> Of the night wind down the vast edges drear
> And naked shingles of the world.

Faith requires deliberate nurturing, for it is not static; it is either increasing or decreasing. Diminution of faith sometimes happens in a "melancholy, long withdrawing roar." At other times its loss occurs in a withering, personal crisis; as when little faith fails to meet a large challenge, and some, ironically, come to see their faith as irrelevant.

1

Poorly defined, faith not only produces little conviction but also is difficult to nurture and increase.

Faith has several specific dimensions. Each facet is important. President Brigham Young illustratively taught that we must have "faith in [Jesus'] name, character, and atonement . . . faith in his Father and in the plan of salvation." Only such faith, said Brigham, will produce steady and enduring "obedience to the requirements of the Gospel."[1] Therefore this book's early chapters focus on President Young's helpful and instructive definition. Since faith's several facets are interactive and interdependent, the boundary lines between chapters will be blurred at times.

Obviously, real faith in Jesus (described in chapters 1 and 2) involves much more than an intellectual acknowledgment or even an appreciative admiration of Him. Do we, for instance, really have faith in Jesus' atonement, or do we merely like His magnificent Sermon on the Mount? Do we like Jesus because He is especially nice, or do we worship Him as the creator of the universe and our perfect Savior? Likewise, can we really expect to develop strong faith in a Being about whose character, purposes, and personality we have little understanding?

Does our faith falter in life's stressful situations simply because we are not "settled" with regard to Father's plan of salvation? (See chapter 3.) Or do we doubt simply because we are not sufficiently "grounded" as to the Lord's supernal character, including His perfect love of us: "Why is He letting this happen to me?"

The manifestations of little faith are many. Some *believe in* the existence of God but do not really *believe Him*—as when, for example, He says of His capacity, "I am able to do mine own work" (2 Nephi 27:20–21). Such people unfortunately are unclear about God's purposes and are likewise uncertain of His capacity to achieve them.

Some, for instance, accept the existence of God but not the existence of His plan of salvation: He is "there," but "why?"

Some are impressed with aspects of Jesus' character but not with how the uniqueness of that character necessarily underwrote the great atonement. Others have a generalized faith in God's overall purposes but are frustrated and irritated with its tactical dimensions, such as God's particularized timing as especially applied to them. But how can we question God's timing without questioning His omniscience? (See D&C 64:32.)

A lack of faith may simply reflect conceptual inadequacy, eyes that are unable to view "things as they really are" (Jacob 4:13).

Increasing our faith, therefore, requires decreasing, one by one, whatever our personal equivocations, reservations, and hesitations are in each of the specific dimensions of faith—those spiritual weaknesses that impede our finally surrendering to the Lord in full faith. By so doing we "perfect that which is lacking in [our] faith" (1 Thessalonians 3:10).

With little faith, for example, we may actually acknowledge God's past blessings but still fear that He will not deliver us in a present situation. Or we may trust that God will finally deliver us but fear He will do so only after a severe trial which we desperately do not want! Such a severe trial may have been in God's plans all along, but it certainly is not in ours! We don't like negative surprises.

Inwardly and anxiously we may worry, too, that an omniscient and loving God sees more stretch in us than we feel we have. Hence when God is actually lifting us up, we may feel He is letting us down.

The challenge of increasing our faith deepens still further when we realize we live in an age ever more distant from Jesus' mortal messiahship and His great atonement. The erosive passage of time has an effect especially on those who already have little faith. F. W. Farrar observed that "nearly two thousand years have passed away, and . . . the brightness of historical events is apt to fade, and even their very outline to be obliterated, as they sink into the 'dark backward and abysm of time.'"[2] Thus we seem to have reached a time, foreseen by some earnest young men in 1912, "when Christianity would have to struggle for a hearing in a world where most would regard it not as untrue or even as unthinkable, but simply ir-relevant."[3] No wonder the renewing and refreshing restora-tion of the gospel was so urgently needed! (See chapter 4.)

As we try to increase faith, we soon see, too, how erosive the effects of the world are. Jesus, who knows the salvational demographics and foresaw the overall ebb and flow, said: "Wide is the gate, and broad is the way, that leadeth to de-struction, and many there be which go in thereat: . . . and narrow is the way, which leadeth unto life, and few there be that find it (Matthew 7:13–14).

No wonder, as well, given the intensification of the factors causing an erosion of faith in the last days, that the Lord has promised to shorten those concluding days for the sake of the elect (see Matthew 24:22).

We are told straightforwardly that we cannot please God "without faith" (see Hebrews 11:6). This is not an arbitrary re-quirement. Since "without faith" we cannot go home to Him, how could a loving Father be pleased with faithless children? He wants us to come home!

Jesus once asked a haunting question: "When the Son of man cometh, shall he find faith on the earth?" (Luke 18:8.) Much later, the resurrected Jesus responded to that question in his 1831 declaration about the Restoration having come so that "faith might also increase in the earth" (D&C 1:21).

Yet how could faith in God increase without an increased understanding of Him and His purposes—all of which the Restoration brought? How could more individuals "speak in the name of God" (D&C 1:20) except they first know His name, understand its implications, and bear His authority?

The Restoration, partially explored in chapters 4 and 5, constituted a vitally needed and reassuring renewal "in the last days," when "scoffers" tauntingly say, "Where is the promise of His coming? . . . All things continue as they were from the beginning of the creation." (2 Peter 3:3, 4.) The promised "times of refreshing" (Acts 3:19) did come, however, bringing a much needed restoration of God's words and ordinances. (See chapter 4.)

The lessons of history concerning faith are deeply relevant to the present. For instance, some of His early disciples found Christ's claim as to His unique role too much. They "walked no more with [Jesus]" (John 6:66, see also chapter 6) when their little faith in Him failed. These fair-weather friends had just eaten hungrily of the miraculous loaves, but still they rejected Jesus' declarations of His divinity as the Bread of Life! Once again, experiencing miracles is no substitute for nurturing daily faith.

Other early disciples, however, trusted, saying, "We believe and are sure that thou art [the] Christ" (John 6:69). Apparently in between were certain loyal followers of John the Baptist. Impressed with Jesus' "works" but still uncertain, they asked if He was really the Messiah, "or do we look for another?" (Matthew 11:3.) Uncertainty about Jesus' true identity thus caused equivocations, hesitations, and reservations.

Defining moments for some back then proved to be sad and separating moments, just as similar sifting moments occur among Jesus' followers today. The acceptance or nonacceptance of His doctrines separates people quickly, but so does obedience to His ordinances. Hence chapter 5 focuses on having faith in these sacred ordinances.

The lack of faith shows up in so many specific and daily ways: failure to pay a full tithing; failure to wear the holy temple garments as promised; refusal to work meekly at making a marriage succeed or a family happier; resentment at personal trials; trying to serve the Lord without offending the devil; being willing to serve the Lord, but only in an advisory capacity; following worldly ways, if only moderately; neglecting prayer; neglecting holy scriptures; neglecting neighbors; neglecting sacrament meetings; neglecting temple attendance; and on and on. Inadequate faith simply cannot successfully masquerade as strong faith for long without being challenged.

5

The equivocations will inevitably emerge. Sufficient unto each day and season of life are the tests of faith. (See chapter 6.)

The quiet and steady decrease of faith leads to a surrendering to the world. When that happens there are no white flags or formal, public ceremonies marking such subjugation. The adversary cleverly does not insist on these ceremonies so long as the results are what he desires.

A few "sell out" directly, like Judas. Thirty pieces of silver are not necessary if a little notoriety will suffice.

There are many more who are honorable individuals but are simply "not valiant" in their testimony of Jesus. Being valiant includes having sufficient faith in Jesus to supply the courage and endurance necessary to move toward becoming more like Him—moving toward mercy and away from vengeance, toward love and away from hate, toward patience and away from impatience and irritability, toward meekness and away from pride.

There is no way to move in those much-desired directions, however, if at the same time we are pandering to the praise of the world. The natural man listens with such a thirsty ear for the approving roar of the crowd. He needs no encouragement to be "of the world," because he is already so much "in the world." Unless the natural man is "put off" (Mosiah 3:19) he will finally put us down. Only when he is put off do we "come off conqueror" (D&C 10:5).

Hence the Savior's dual requirement is for self-denial and for taking up our cross daily (see Luke 9:23). Self-denial commences the cure, because the natural man or woman constantly wants the wrong things—things which will harm both self and others. This denial establishes direction. Then, taking up the cross daily brings momentum, moving one toward spiritual maturity and its reinforcing rewards. (See chapter 7.)

The rewards of this journey are many. When seeing daily life with the eye of faith, we see God, mortality, others, and even the universe very differently and more richly. And we are "glad"! (See Ether 12:19.) The eye of faith allows us entry into the sun-drenched uplands of reality, where we can better see "things as they really are" and "really will be" (Jacob 4:13).

Without faith, however, we simply "cannot see afar off." Whether we are viewing man's eventual prospects in the plan of salvation or the other "things of the Spirit of God [which] . . . are spiritually discerned," faith is essential. (2 Peter 1:9; 1 Corinthians 2:14.)

At present we are required to "walk by faith, not by sight" (2 Corinthians 5:7). We can finally "overcome by faith" (D&C 76:53), which is the only real and lasting form of personal triumph. Yes, the later day will come when "every knee shall bow and every tongue confess that Jesus is the Christ." C. S. Lewis wondered just how much credit kneeling then will bring, when it will no longer be possible to stand up! Practical, spiritual Brigham Young noted, "There is no saving faith merely upon the principle of believing or acknowledging a fact."[4]

Real faith, operational in daily life, does not consist merely in giving "arid assent" to some abstract theology. To be made "alive in Christ because of our faith" (2 Nephi 25:25) pertains not only to faith in the later resurrection but also to having sufficient faith to lead a vibrant, daily life here in mortality.

As we inventory whatever our personal hesitations, reservations, or equivocations are, it is better to acknowledge them honestly while meekly indicating to God that, though we understand somewhat the doctrine of faith, we need help in practicing it. "Lord, help thou my unbelief" (Mark 9:24). It is better to acknowledge too that comparatively we understand more about *why* faith is important than *how* to increase faith.

Since a better understanding of it increases our faith, why do we leave unexamined the application of the plan of salvation, with its many and specific implications for our "daily" lives? (Luke 9:23.) For instance, we struggle over when our faithful importuning should end and our acceptance of a "thorn in the flesh" should begin. We should not be surprised that achieving such a balance is difficult, because faith is a process and not a passive, mental state.

Given real faith, significant things happen in that unfolding process. Paul sets forth an especially powerful litany of what has happened "by faith," ranging from the creation of worlds to the building of an ark (see Hebrews 11). Each of us can and should have his or her own litany, to be "added upon" as life progresses.

The more specifically we focus on the objects of our faith, such as President Young outlined them,[5] the more specific will be the increase in our faith, and the more beneficial the process will be. If the focal points are not clear, however, we will find our faith weak, since we will be either unfocused or "looking beyond the mark" (Jacob 4:14).

Since faith, then, is both a principle and a process, if our faith is not increasing it is probably shrinking. In that case we are likely to become "wearied and faint in [our] minds" (Hebrews 12:3). "Looking unto Jesus" (Hebrews 12:2) therefore involves looking to Him in specific ways, such as by comprehending more about His names, His atonement, and His character.

Christ, His atonement, and His character—these are where we rightly commence.

CHAPTER

1

Faith in Jesus' Name and Atonement

Each of the Savior's names implies so much! The name *Jesus* denotes "God's help" and "Savior." The name *Christ* means "Anointed One," "Messiah." We are to have faith in those names and in their implications for all mankind and for us personally.[1] These names are profound, especially when compared to the understandable but understated appellations "the carpenter's son" or "Jesus of Nazareth." Designations by vocation or location are far too provincial when describing the Lord of the universe!

Not understanding who Jesus really is by title and role inevitably sets up a lack of gratitude for His astonishing atonement. If we do not regard Him highly enough to pay heed to His words about *who* He is, we will pay less heed to *what* He says and requires of us. The resulting diminution of regard and comprehension will result in little faith. What "think [we] of Christ" inevitably determines His operative relevancy for our lives.

Contrariwise, a positive and interactive multiplier effect flows from having faith in Christ as the anointed Messiah, the

King and Deliverer. This facet of faith complements faith in His Father, who chose and anointed Jesus as the Redeemer of mankind; and this in turn begets faith in the Father's plan of salvation.

Therefore, defining Jesus, as some do, as a great moral teacher—and He was clearly the greatest—just won't suffice. Without full faith in Jesus as mankind's rescuing Messiah, we also will lack faith in His capacity to rescue us individually and to help us daily. Besides, how can one consistently regard Jesus as a great moral teacher, and therefore truthful and honorable, if one does not accept Jesus' statements about His true identity?

As it was anciently, so it is in our skeptical day. The "great question" remains—"Is there really a redeeming Christ?" (See Alma 34:5.)

There is!

Christ is in reality the Lord of the universe, who created "worlds without number" for the Father's "own purpose" (Moses 1:33; see also Hebrews 1:2). Those unnourished by such gospel truths, however, will hold a smaller view of Jesus and a smaller view of man's eventual prospects. Some speak wistfully, perhaps hopefully, of "whatever god may be."

In fact, Paul declared, expansively but correctly, "in [Christ] all things hold together" (RSV, Colossians 1:17). Jesus' role as the creator of the cosmos and His rescuing and emancipating atonement reflect how He holds all the everlasting things together. "By him, and through him, and of him, the worlds are and were created, and the inhabitants thereof are begotten sons and daughters unto God" (D&C 76:24; see also Moses 1:33; Hebrews 1:2).

In His post-resurrection pronouncements and instructions, Christ does not mention the details of His suffering: the scourging; the crown of thorns; the proffered vinegar and gall; being spit upon, struck, and mocked. Instead, Jesus instructively confides His chief concern, which was whether, having partaken of the bitter cup, He might have failed to finish His work! His mental, physical, and spiritual suffering was so intense that as He expressed it, it

> caused myself, even God, the greatest of all, to tremble because of pain, and to bleed at every pore, and to suffer both body and spirit—and *would that I might not drink the bitter cup, and shrink*—

Yet He persisted.

> . . . and I partook and finished my preparations unto the children of men (D&C 19:18–19, italics added).

The deep feelings inherent in Jesus' use of the word *would* may be better appreciated by reflecting on how He used that same word on another occasion: "O Jerusalem, Jerusalem, thou that killest the prophets, and stonest them which are sent unto thee, how often *would* I have gathered thy children together, even as a hen gathereth her chickens under her wings, and ye *would* not!" (Matthew 23:37, italics added; see also D&C 43:24.)

Deep desires can produce a confluence of powerful emotions. "And it came to pass that I [Nephi] . . . said in my heart: Never at any time have I shed the blood of man. And I shrunk and would that I might not slay him." (1 Nephi 4:10.)

The significance of Jesus' use of the word *shrink* is thus further underscored. There should be no doubt about what *shrink* means: "And it came to pass that when the men of Moroni saw the fierceness and the anger of the Lamanites, they were about to shrink and flee from them" (Alma 43:48).

Facing our own small-scale "fierceness" can cause real fear, producing a deep desire to "shrink and flee"! It is merciful for all mortals that Jesus did not shrink nor flee, even amid "the fierceness of the wrath of Almighty God" (D&C 76:107; 88:106). As He took upon Himself our sins, standing graciously in our stead, He thus felt severe, divine reproach, which "hath broken my heart" (Psalm 69:20). The Hebrew word for Jesus' being "bruised" in the process of the Atonement means "to be crushed" (see Isaiah 53:5). The atoning "man of sorrows" denotes both physical and spiritual sorrow and pain. Being "acquainted with grief" includes familiarity with "sickness" (Isaiah 53:3; see also Alma 7:11, 12; Matthew 8:17). Yet amid the engulfing avalanche of anguish, Jesus did not shrink or flee.

President John Taylor explained that Jesus' doing the will of the Father "was a hard thing for Him to do. Did you ever think of it? When He found the accumulated weight of the sins of the world rolling upon His head, His feelings were so intense that He sweat great drops of blood. Could I tell it, or could you? No. Suffice it to say that He bore the sins of the world, and, when laboring under the pressure of those intense agonies, He exclaimed, 'Father, if it be possible, let this cup pass.' But it was not possible. It was the decree of God."[2]

Elder Erastus Snow spoke of Jesus' agony being further added upon when the Father's power "withdrew itself *measurably* from [Jesus]. . . . he was led to exclaim in his last agony upon the cross, My God, my God, why hast thou forsaken me? The Father did not deign to answer; the time had not yet come to explain it and tell him. But after a little, when he passed the ordeal, made the sacrifice, and by the power of God was raised from the dead, then all was clear, all was explained and comprehended fully. It was necessary that the Father should thus *measurably* forsake his Son."[3]

Jesus' "Why," framed in His forsakenness cry, reflected His full faith in the Father even amid the perplexing anguish when, as Brigham Young expressed it, "the Father withdrew Himself, withdrew His Spirit, and cast a vail over him. . . . and He then plead with the Father not to forsake Him."[4]

Likewise, we "receive no witness until after the trial of [our] faith" (Ether 12:6). Though on a much smaller scale than the Savior's, our trials ensure that we too surely will "measurably" experience anguish. Our "whys" may not be immediately responded to, either. Only later will things be "comprehended fully."

During the process of the agonizing atonement, Jesus suffered "both body and spirit" (D&C 19:18). The uniquely torturous interplay of His physical and spiritual anguish produced enormous suffering and pain! In fact, King Benjamin declared Jesus' anguish would be "more than man can suffer" (Mosiah 3:7).

Moreover, Jesus' pain was fully inclusive and comprehensive. Surely He was thereby fully "acquainted with grief," because "he suffered the pain of all men," indeed, "the pains of every living creature, both men, women, and children, who belong to the family of Adam" (Isaiah 53:3, 5; D&C 18:11; 2 Nephi 9:21). It will take faith to "finish" our own assigned tasks amid whatever grief, pain, and infirmities may be.

No wonder that in the Garden of Gethsemane Jesus began to be "sore amazed," meaning "awestruck," "astounded," and "astonished." Jesus was also "very heavy," meaning "depressed," "dejected," and in "anguish." (Mark 14:33.)

In a messianic psalm David spoke about Jesus' heartbreaking circumstances, including His being totally *alone* in the awful process! "Reproach hath broken my heart; and I am full of heaviness: and I looked for some to take pity, but there was none; and for comforters, but I found none. They gave me also gall for my meat; and in my thirst they gave me vinegar to drink." (Psalm 69:20–21.)

Jesus always deserved and always had the Father's full approval. But when He took our sins upon Him, of divine necessity required by justice He experienced instead "the fierceness of the wrath of Almighty God" (D&C 76:107; 88:106).

Irony, the hard crust on the bread of adversity, was pervasively present in the suffering of the Lord of the universe, who was treated so grossly and unjustly. "And the world, because of their iniquity, shall judge him to be a thing of naught; wherefore they scourge him, and he suffereth it; and they smite him, and he suffereth it. Yea, they spit upon him, and he suffereth it." Why did He endure it all? "Because of his loving kindness and his long-suffering towards the children of men." (1 Nephi 19:9.)

Jesus' being "very heavy" or "depressed" ensured His perfect empathy—born of actual experience—for all of us when we feel overwhelmed or depressed (see Mark 14:33; Psalm 69:20). Christ "descended below all things, in that he comprehended all things" (D&C 88:6; see also 122:8).

His suffering thereby permitted Jesus to "be filled with mercy," because He knows "according to the flesh how to succor his people according to their infirmities" (Alma 7:12; see also Hebrews 5:8; Matthew 8:17). Alma and Paul agreed: Jesus' capacity to help was fully perfected through His supernal obedience. Jesus thus understands the full range of human suffering personally and perfectly. He also understands temptation as only our most righteous Lord can: "For in that he himself hath suffered being tempted, he is able to succour them that are tempted" (Hebrews 2:18).

Our experiences, though on an infinitesimally smaller scale, include at times both mental and physical pain. Interesting examples on this lesser scale abound about interactive pain, when mental anguish produces physical pain and vice versa.

King Benjamin pointed out that all of us are "subject to all manner of infirmities in body and mind" (Mosiah 2:11). While "men are, that they might have joy," sadness and discouragement are well represented in the mortal experience. Anciently, one group were "about to turn back" because their "hearts were depressed" (Alma 26:27). Turning back is a form of shrinking. Another group was "depressed in body as well as in spirit" (Alma 56:16).

The sons of Mosiah "did suffer much, both in body and in mind." Physical suffering from hunger, thirst, and fatigue may be accompanied by "much labor in the spirit," denoting the confluence of emotions in such real struggles. (Alma 17:5.)

When we are amid pain, faith in God's plan of salvation includes faith in His love, capacity, timing, tutoring, and purposes, "for [God] doeth not anything save it be for the benefit of the world" (2 Nephi 26:24).

The central purpose in God's declared work and glory is to "bring to pass the immortality and eternal life of man" (Moses 1:39). Eternal life is God's "greatest gift," made possible by His Son, Jesus (see D&C 14:7). It, along with personal immortality, is likewise made possible through Jesus' atonement.

Thus we see the reassuring interplay between the several facets of faith—faith in Jesus' names, His atonement, His character, and His Father's plan of salvation. All are bound up together, making possible the forming of a sturdy, interlocking faith. In order to increase faith, however, one must increase the tensile strength in all of several facets of faith.

Hence the constant need to let the doctrine of faith with its several dimensions and many implications settle into the marrow of our souls. But if we do not face and erase our reservations and hesitations, tutoring events may be needed. Being spurred by such events, though unasked for, can move us to increase our faith.

A Book of Mormon prophet asked, rhetorically, "Why not speak of the atonement?" (Jacob 4:12.) But when we do speak of the Atonement, is it in the most helpful ways? Do we actually "liken" the implications of the Atonement "unto ourselves"? Bruce C. Hafen wrote insightfully:

> I grieve for those who, in their admirable and sometimes blindly dogged sense of personal responsibility, believe that, in the quest for eternal life, the Atonement is there only to help big-time sinners, and that they, as everyday Mormons who just have to try harder, must "make it" on their own. The truth is not that *we* must make it on *our* own, but that *he* will make us *his* own.
>
> . . . The scriptures suggest that the heresy of salvation by grace alone also applies to the personal developmental process.

15

Thus, we will not be blessed with hope and charity and eternal life only for the asking. Rather, we must do the very best *we* can—even if that may not seem terribly impressive compared to a standard of flawless perfection. The important thing is that we *can* qualify, despite failures, bad judgments, wrong turns, and limited strength.[5]

Expressing a similar view, Stephen E. Robinson observed:

To have faith in Jesus Christ is not merely to believe that he is who he says he is. It is not merely to believe *in* Christ; we must also *believe* Christ. Both as a bishop and as a teacher, I have heard several variations on a theme of doubt. Some have said, "Bishop, I've sinned too horribly. I'll be active in the Church, and I hope for some reward. But I couldn't ever hope to be exalted after what I've done." Others have said, "I'm weak and imperfect. I don't have all the talents that Brother Jones (or Sister Smith) does. I'll never be the bishop (or the Relief Society president). I'm just average. I expect my reward in eternity will be a little lower than theirs." . . .

. . . It is those who *don't* have the righteousness that God has—but who hunger and thirst after it—who are blessed, for if that is the desire of their hearts, the Lord will help them achieve it. . . .

. . . Many of us are trying to save ourselves, holding the atonement of Jesus Christ at arm's distance and saying, "When I've perfected myself, then I'll be worthy of the Atonement." But that's not how it works. That's like saying, "I won't take the medicine until I'm well. I'll be worthy of it then."[6]

Mercifully the Lord speaks of His gifts given not only to those who keep all His commandments but also to "him that seeketh so to do" (D&C 46:9).

Do we ponder the other implications of Jesus' atonement? On one occasion, five members of the Quorum of the Twelve were informally discussing the Lord's impressive and revealing words about His atonement, as expressed in section 19 of the Doctrine and Covenants. When asked, President Howard W.

Hunter promptly and meekly said that the most impressive thing to him about those several verses was that suffering "Jesus gave all the glory to the Father."

The Atonement is full of exemplifying as well as redeeming things about the character of Jesus that can be "likened" to us. Jesus did not mention His scourging or the disapproving spittle which fell upon Him. These things appear to have been incidental to Him. Instead, He meekly focused on transcendent things.

Thus the Atonement not only rescues us but also exemplifies Jesus' character. His character can guide us, beacon-like, in the midst of our own afflictions, since these constitute the necessary crucible for the further refining and confirmation of our own character.

Christ's atonement simply would not have been possible without His splendid character! He not only had the integrity and submissiveness to finish doing the Father's will, but, just as He had premortally promised, He then meekly and gladly gave all the glory to the Father (see Moses 4:2; D&C 19:19). There is such majesty in Jesus' meekness and such eloquent example in His refusal ever to self-aggrandize. Even in His healings, there was no boasting: "*Thy* faith hath made thee whole" (Mark 5:34, italics added).

The Father's plan required, and He provided, a Deliverer with the unique character to deliver.

CHAPTER

2

Faith in Jesus' Character

 The character of Jesus is resplendently and constantly shown in all the accounts we have of Him. In fact, it is precisely because of the matchless luminosity of his character that Jesus truly qualifies as the Light of the World. It is by means of His light that we should view everything else! When our view is so illuminated, we can truly see "things as they really are" (Jacob 4:13). Little wonder that the more we understand and experience God's and Jesus' love for *us*, the more we want to please them, to be more like them, and to be with them.

The more emulative faith we have in Jesus' character, which even during the deepest moments of His suffering was devoid of self-pity, the less likely we are to indulge in disabling self-pity ourselves. The more we know about the character of God and of Jesus, which ensures their desire to help us, and also about their capacity to help us, the more we will have faith that the Lord's "grace is sufficient" to see us through our personal trials and troubles (see Ether 12:26–27). The greater our personal anxiety or agony, the more earnestly we need to seek the desperately needed, helping grace!

As we develop further faith in the integrity and the interweaving of divine commands, this will simultaneously increase our striving to become "even as [He is]" (3 Nephi 27: 27). Given our awareness of our deficiencies, we may ask, "Does Jesus really think I can become a significantly better person?" The answer is yes! Furthermore, faith in His atonement provides the necessary way for us to repent in order to become better. Otherwise we would be stranded in life's shoals.

The more we contemplate God's character, the more we understand that the God who watches over Israel does not sleep, nor does he slumber (see Psalm 121:4). If there are what appear to us to be ambiguities and perplexities, God has, long beforehand, taken all these into account. He has made "ample provision"[1] for His purposes to be achieved fully. We will not be exempted from these uncertainties, however, nor will we always see the end from the beginning. But knowing adequately of the divine character and plans, we can proceed anyway, for "we know that all things work together for good to them that love God, to them who are the called according to his purpose" (Romans 8:28).

Faith permits us to "hold up [our] light that it may shine unto the world," while remembering that Jesus said, "I am the light which ye shall hold up" (3 Nephi 18:24). As we both testify of Him and strive to replicate His way of life in our own, we are reverently and respectfully holding Him up to proper human view.

"From the beginning" Jesus "suffered the will of the Father in all things" (3 Nephi 11:11). Jesus always let His will be swallowed up in the will of the Father (see Mosiah 15:7).[2] Christ was the perfect Son, as His constant submission sanctified His already remarkable, divine character. John Taylor observed:

Now, I will consider the character of Jesus. . . . It was absolutely necessary that he should pass through this state, and be subject to all the weaknesses of the flesh—that he should also be subjected to the buffetings of Satan the same as we are, and pass through all the trials incident to humanity, and thereby comprehend the weakness and the true character of human nature, with all its faults and foibles, that we might have a faithful High Priest that would know how to deliver those that are tempted; and hence one of the Apostles, in speaking of him, says, "For we have not a High Priest which cannot be touched with the feelings of our infirmities, but was in all points tempted like as we are, yet without sin."[3]

In even the seemingly small episodes in Jesus' ministry there are large lessons. Each one reflects His remarkable character and His divine discernment about how important it is that faith be built on correct doctrines.

In fact, Jesus perceptively warned His disciples against the "leaven," or doctrine, of the Pharisees and the Sadducees (see Matthew 16:6). Jesus' concerns would have included how their false doctrines led to false behavior, as in the ways in which Pharisees were ceremonial and proud. They expected an earthly paradise and a triumph in this world of a Messiah who would overthrow the hated Gentile rule. The doctrines in the plan of salvation do not so provide, however, since Christ's kingdom is not of this world (see John 18:36). The Sadducees denied the existence of angels and the preexistence; and not having the complete writings of Moses, they did not believe in a literal resurrection (see Acts 23:8). This haunting incompleteness regarding the words of Moses was confirmed by the Lord, who said: "And now, Moses, my son, I will speak unto thee concerning this earth upon which thou standest; and thou shalt write the things which I shall speak. And in a day when the children of men shall esteem my words as naught and take many of them from the book which thou shalt write, behold, I will raise up another like unto thee; and they shall be had again among the children of men—among as many as shall believe." (Moses 1:40–41.)

No wonder a restoration was needed! No wonder the full

scriptural record God has given us is so vital, lest we be affected by the "leaven" of today's erroneous philosophies. The philosophy of the Sadducees may have contributed to the tendency (after "the Apostles fell asleep") to explain away the physical resurrection, as the spread of Greek culture in Israel hastened the subsequent Hellenization of the early Church.

Paul's experience in Athens showed the mind-set of Greek philosophy (see Acts 17). His intellectually curious audience asked about "this new doctrine. . . . for thou bringest strange things to our ears." Then when Paul spoke of the Living God and the resurrection, he was "mocked" for seeming to set "forth . . . strange gods." (See Acts 18–20, 29, 32.)

Some defined matter as intrinsically evil, an idea representing both Greek and Oriental thought. Hence, if the body constitutes a "dark jail" from which we should seek to escape, why desire a resurrection?[4] This view contrasts sharply with modern revelation which declares that only when the resurrected body and the individual spirit are inseparably connected can there be a "fulness of joy" (D&C 93:33; see also 88:15–16; 138:17). Besides, God used matter to create this earth so it could "be inhabited," after which He "saw every thing that he had made, and, behold, it was very good"—not evil! (Isaiah 45:18; Genesis 1:31.)

Furthermore, some questioned worshipping a God who suffers. One modern scholar observed that "the human sufferings of Jesus . . . were felt as an embarrassment in the face of pagan criticism."[5] Thus many Greeks considered Christ and what He stood for as "foolishness" (1 Corinthians 1:23).

The Apostle John denounced anti-Christs who taught that Jesus hadn't really come "in the flesh" (1 John 4:3), implying that Jesus' bodily appearance was an illusion designed to accommodate mortal incapacities (see John 1:1–3, 14). Another Hellenistic form of "looking beyond the mark" was interpreting clear, historical events as allegorical. These early denials of Jesus' historicity are replicated in our day.

Reason, the Greek philosophical tradition, dominated, then

supplanted, reliance on revelation, an outcome probably hastened by well-intentioned Christians wishing to bring their beliefs into the mainstream of contemporary culture. Historian Will Durant wrote: "Christianity did not destroy paganism; it adopted it. The Greek mind, dying, came to a transmigrated life."[6]

By the middle of the second century, things had changed dramatically. Another scholar wrote of how the theological furniture had been significantly rearranged in ways which reflected a Hellenized Christianity.[7]

Jesus' warning, therefore, against the leaven of the Pharisees and Sadducees, in a sense was a generic warning against these same doctrinal symptoms, though these two religious parties soon disappeared from the landscape of human history.

Paul worried about Church members who in his time "swerved" from true doctrines or who missed the mark (see 1 Timothy 1:6). With prophetic anticipation, Jacob wrote of the related dangers of "looking beyond the mark" (Jacob 4:14). When people do not have full scriptural records, harsh consequences can ensue. In one instance in the Book of Mormon, a malnourished group denied the existence of their creator (see Omni 1:17). In a similar situation, some believed neither in a resurrection nor in the coming of Christ, not understanding the word of God (see Mosiah 26:2–5).

If our approach is superficial, we may be unnoticing of the profound implications for us of the words which inform us of Jesus' character and that He suffered "temptations of every kind" but "gave no heed unto them" (Alma 7:11; D&C 20:22). Given His keen intellect and unique sensitivity, the Savior would surely have noticed each and every temptation. Yet marvelously He "gave no heed" to them. His character is without flaw, so we can trust Him fully. He also knows our flaws and how to help us remove them.

It is our giving heed to temptations by dallying over them and by anticipating, savoring, and recycling them that get us into trouble. Jesus' character is such that He was consistently decisive and dismissive as to temptation and sin. There is no equivocation in Him regarding evil. He and His Father can make no allowance for sin (see D&C 1:31)—because of the terrible toll sin exacts from the happiness of all those they love.

We mortals, on the other hand, tend to tolerate our own little clusters of sin. We rationalize that we can dismiss these whenever we really want to. The trouble is that these "squatters" come to have "rights," too. By means of their persistent presence, they take over more than we ever intended; whereas to give no heed means to give no foothold, however small. To delay their eviction is, in effect, to "heed" and accommodate the temptation.

Being meek and lowly in character, majestic Jesus was uninterested in power per se. He repeatedly refused to use His power inappropriately even to lessen His awful suffering during His temptations and atonement. He did not manipulate—even to further His righteous purposes for mankind. For example, previous to Gethsemane and the Crucifixion Pilate and Herod had been "at enmity," yet in response to the crisis which Jesus' presence created, they "made friends together" (Luke 23:12). Opportunities doubtless existed for Jesus to take advantage of their temporary alliance in order to please them. Thereby He might have reduced at least some of His suffering if He had been willing to shrink, even partially, from going through with all of the full agonies of the Atonement (see D&C 19:18, 19).

After all, Pilate found no fault with Jesus. Herod, too, was probably reachable, having been desirous "to see [Jesus] of a long season," hoping "to have seen some miracle done by him" (Luke 23:8–9). Yet, standing before Herod, fully aware of the ruler's expectations and with a chance to please him, Jesus "answered him nothing" (Luke 23:9; see also Mosiah 14:7). There would be no demonstration to purchase even slight amelioration. Jesus gave no consolation to inquiring Pilate either. Jesus' integrity was never for sale. There was such strength in His meekness, whereas a lesser individual would have gladly seized upon any opportunity for relief. But anointed Jesus' character was such that He would not shrink from His appointed and agonizing task.

It was to be an "infinite atonement," necessarily complete with infinite suffering (2 Nephi 9:7; Alma 34:12; see also Mosiah 3:7). There would be no equivocation in the face of the suffering. Jesus' character so guaranteed.

Drenched in deep and, to us, unimaginable personal suffering at the time of His arrest in Gethsemane, Jesus might have shrouded Himself in self-pity, reducing His capacity to think of others at all. Instead, empathetic Jesus carefully restored the severed ear of a hostile guard (see Luke 22:50–51). Christ's way was not the way of the sword (see Matthew 26:52). Even in the deepest duress, He did not hesitate or equivocate.

There is record of only a few sentences spoken from the cross by suffering Jesus. One thoughtful utterance assured that His mother, Mary, would be cared for by the Apostle John. Another sentence reassured a pleading thief by Jesus' side. Even while Jesus was literally providing salvation for all mankind, the perfect Shepherd simultaneously reached out to individuals.

When you and I suffer, however, we sometimes tend to pass it along. Or, if overcome with self-pity, we simply ignore others, saying, in effect, "I've got all I can handle with my own problems."

His character is such that we can always approach our Lord, knowing He is not preoccupied with problems of His own. From the viewpoint of our lower ways, Jesus' vast and consuming responsibilities offered a viable excuse for focusing only on the macro, on universal duties at hand. Nevertheless, Jesus took time to personalize. The Nephite Twelve, for instance, were interviewed by Him "one by one" (3 Nephi 28:1). Clearly, with His perfect discernment, He knew beforehand what their individual desires were. It was not that he lacked information; rather, they needed individual affection and expression. So the resurrected Lord of the universe gave each an individual audience and choice. Someday, perhaps, we shall know more about those personal interviews.

Though universal in His dominions, Jesus never worried, as some of us do, about audience size. He was, for example, gently disclosing of His true identity to a solitary, believing woman of Samaria: "The woman saith unto him, I know that Messias cometh, which is called Christ: when he is come, he will tell us all things. Jesus saith unto her, I that speak unto thee am he." (John 4:25–26.)

The personalization was the same with imprisoned Paul, who was visited, reassured, and challenged by no less a personage than the resurrected Lord of the universe. Another audience of one! "And the night following the Lord stood by him, and said, Be of good cheer, Paul: for as thou hast testified of me in Jerusalem, so must thou bear witness also at Rome" (Acts 23:11).

Jesus' perfect sensitivity in communicating with individuals was shown in His response to the tenth leper, who was grateful enough to return. Appreciatively, but penetratingly, Jesus replied, "Where are the nine?" (Luke 17:17.) He did not scold the grateful one. When you and I experience ingratitude, however, we sometimes unload our frustration on those who deserve it least.

To the more accountable mother of James and John, who wrongly craved next-world status for her fine sons, Jesus gave less mild reproof—"Ye know not what ye ask"—further indicating that the Father had already made certain determinations (see Matthew 20:22).

Of the previously confident Peter, who faltered briefly, Jesus pointedly asked three times, "Lovest thou me?" (John 21:15–17.) Peter's subsequent heart-wrenching but heart-cleansing responses were apparently a spiritual necessity. After all, Peter, who knew much more, was not the less informed and less accountable tenth leper.

Thus Jesus never shrank from giving needed counsel, yet

He always took account of the varied receiving capacities of others. You and I, by contrast, sometimes devastate the tender and leave the arrogant unfazed.

The post-doctoral disciples, it seems, often have the toughest curriculum. President John Taylor observed that sometimes "God tries people according to the position they occupy."[8] Similarly, Joseph Smith reportedly observed that "the higher the authority, the greater the difficulty of the station."[9]

We sometimes use our talents and capacities to put someone down, while Jesus sought to lift others up, both proximately and ultimately. Jesus, the brightest and most gifted of all intellects ever to grace this planet, but also the meekest, neither sought to dominate others nor to prosper nor to conquer "according to His genius" (Alma 30:17).

Searching the scriptures provides reason after reason in case after case for having full faith in Jesus' character. If we truly contemplate that character, we are drawn to emulate, refusing to risk becoming "wearied and faint in [our] minds" (Hebrews 12:3).

It was Christ's character with His unique combination of celestial attributes which brought Him to and got Him through Gethsemane and Calvary. We less reliables can always rely upon Him. President Brigham Young inquired: "Do we rely upon Him, and are we acquainted with His character in the least degree? Have we any knowledge of Him? Let us answer these questions in our own minds, that we may ascertain whether we do delight to bow down before Him to ask for the things which we need, and seek unto Him for His Spirit to guide us, and preserve us from all danger, that we may not wander into . . . forbidden paths and fall out by the way, but be kept constantly in the narrow path which leads to life ever-. lasting."[10]

Since all the laws and the prophets hang upon the first and second commandments (see Matthew 22:35–40), our keeping of those two great commandments is the biggest and most constant challenge. If, however, after all they have done for us, we do not have enough faith to love the Father and Jesus, or if we deny the divinity of the Lord who so agonizingly ransomed us, whatever else in life we honorably accomplish it will not qualify us for eternal association with them.

Thus, by looking unto Jesus and His character we are determining just how extensively we will "consider Him." Alas, if "even after all this," some still "consider him a man" (Mosiah 3:9), then sadness and despair will surely follow them.

Whether one is so enfeebled by unwise relaxation of Jesus' demonstrated standards or by needless exhaustion from lack of spiritual nourishment, the results will be the same. One will despond and become fainthearted.

Yet faith is never lost without leaving a valid record of its past presence. Its tracings, like it or not, show the bounds of previous belief and tell of our present accountability. These tracings will disclose what we once knew, when we knew it, and how we behaved in reference to it. No present rationalizations can erase past realizations.

There is another powerful reason for becoming informed about the character of Jesus: increased self-understanding. The Prophet Joseph taught, "If men do not comprehend the character of God, they do not comprehend themselves."[11] How can we come to have more of "the mind of Christ" (1 Corinthians 2:16) except by knowing more about Him and His thoughts?

Elder John Taylor taught encouragingly:

> We read that the Savior . . . "Was tempted in all points like unto us, yet without sin; therefore he . . . knows how to deliver those who are tempted." We have our weaknesses, our infirmities, follies, and foibles. It is the intention of the gospel to deliver us from these. . . . If we make any little stumbles the Savior acts not as a foolish, vindictive man, to knock another man down. He is full of kindness, long suffering, and forbearance, and treats everybody with kindness and courtesy. These are the feelings we wish to indulge in and be governed by.[12]

28

If, knowing of Jesus' loving-kindness, we too are developing such, we can work more effectively to overcome our failures. This can occur even while amid "all these things" that are deliberately designed to "give [us] experience" which, though difficult, can be for our everlasting "good" (see D&C 122:7).

Similarly, if we really have sufficient faith to enjoy "faith unto repentance" (Alma 34:17), this in itself dramatically lightens our life loads. Even so, how long it takes us to heave off the heavy burdens of hypocrisy! Perhaps the saddest consequence of little faith is little repentance. The burden of believing seems so heavy, when it is actually the wearying weight of our own sins that we feel. Our spiritual mobility is determined by how much we can jettison, including by putting off the sumo-sized natural man.

If we are serious enough about the gospel, we will let it so change us. All this is part of the hard labor of working out our salvation. Becoming the "manner of men" and women we ought to be by patterning ourselves after Jesus' character spares us from being wearily and incessantly "conformed to this world" (3 Nephi 27:27; Romans 12:2). No wonder our full spiritual development occurs "in process of time."

Lorenzo Snow reflected on the development "in process of time" of the characters of gallant Peter and exemplary Abraham:

> There was the Apostle Peter, for instance, a man valiant for the truth, . . . he told the Savior on a certain occasion that though all men forsook him he would not. But the Savior, foreseeing what would happen, told him that on that same night, before the cock crowed, he would deny him thrice, and he did so. He proved himself unequal for the trial; but afterwards he gained power. . . . And if we could read in detail the life of Abraham, or the lives of other great and holy men, we would doubtless find that their efforts to be righteous were not always crowned with success. Hence we should not be discouraged if we should

be overcome in a weak moment; but, on the contrary, straight-way repent of the error or the wrong we may have committed, and as far as possible repair it, and then seek to God for re-newed strength to go on and do better.[13]

Of all the Father's and Jesus' perfected virtues, the two most to be celebrated in connection with the plan of salvation and the Atonement are their *loving-kindness* and their *long-suffering*, qualities which equipped Jesus to accomplish the Atonement (see 1 Nephi 19:9). These virtues in Him will evoke our everlasting praise. In fact, we will gladly praise His loving-kindness and long-suffering "for ever and ever" (D&C 133:52).

To emulate Jesus by further developing these same quali-ties in ourselves takes daily faith. There is no such thing as spurts of long-suffering. Yet even when proffered, our long-suffering and loving-kindness may not always be appreciated by others; and it may not only go unreciprocated but may even be misread as a weakness.

Our dependence upon God and His character and pur-pose is a reality, whether acknowledged or not. This is one es-pecially vital fact among "things as they really are" (Jacob 4:13). It would be intellectually dishonest for God to let us mortals think otherwise! Furthermore, God's ways are much higher than our ways (see Isaiah 55:8–9). This reality is some-thing which those of us in the foothills of faith should ponder before, in our provinciality, we try to force God's doctrines through the filter of our lower ways. His is an invitation de-signed to lift us up in style as well as in substance.

Jesus seeks to lift people up, and so do His true disciples. This lifting loving-kindness is especially needed in behalf of those whose hands hang down. Such hands are, it seems, un-able even to reach out in hope any more: there have been too many disappointments. Loving-kindness will cause us to no-tice and then to reach for those hands. Loving-kindness also simultaneously verifies to the recipients not only our love for them but their intrinsic worth—especially if we show that what is our duty in this matter is also our delight.

Faith is not, therefore, merely an arid contemplation of Christ, in which we are unanxiously unengaged! One who is "made alive in Christ" (2 Nephi 25:25) is, instead, becoming ever more like Him. Such a disciple is moved to love more, to forgive more, to endure more, and to repent more. Since such character is formed and refined in the crucible of life with its fiery trials, there can be no developmental exemptions! Having faith in Jesus' character, so crucial by itself, complements faith in the Father and in His plan of salvation.

CHAPTER
3

Faith in the Father's Plan of Salvation

All we know of Him and about His character, including the very approach He uses in His plan of happiness, suggests clearly to us that our Heavenly Father is in it for the long haul, for all the right reasons, and with all the right motivations. He is also in it with the right methodology: love unfeigned, long-suffering, and by showing us the way. It is contrary to God's character to dictate to us. Hence some will be lost because of their misuse of moral agency and their lack of faith. Were it otherwise, genuine happiness and growth could not occur. Scientist Alan Hayward wrote of an illustrative experience.

> Suppose for a moment that God made His presence felt all the time—that every action of ours, good or bad, brought an immediate response from Him in the form of reward or punishment. What sort of a world would this be then?
>
> It would resemble, on a grander scale, the dining room of a hotel . . . where I once stayed for a few days. The European owner evidently did not trust his . . . waiters. He would sit on a raised platform at one end of the room, constantly watching

every movement. Goods that might possibly be pilfered, such as tea bags, sugar knobs and even pats of butter or margarine, were doled out by him in quantities just sufficient for the needs of the moment. He would scrutinise every bill like Sherlock Holmes looking for signs of foul play.

The results of all this supervision were painfully obvious. I have stayed in many hotels around the world . . . but never have I met such an unpleasant bunch of waiters as in that hotel. Their master's total lack of trust in them had warped their personalities. As long as he was watching they acted discreetly, but the moment they thought his guard was down they would seize the opportunity to misbehave.

In much the same way, it would ruin our own characters if God's presence were as obvious as that of the [hotel owner]. This would then be a world without trust, without faith, without unselfishness, without love—a world where everybody obeyed God because it paid them to do so. Horrors![1]

But how sustained is our faith in the Father's plan of salvation when we experience personal or family adversity? Or when we see wrenching, widespread human suffering? Especially if either of these continues unrelieved?

Modern communication ensures that we will receive poignant and regular doses of graphic, global suffering. Our scale of such awareness is something earlier generations never knew. Granted, we still see only a very small fraction of all that God sees, but the tiny fraction is part of the needless suffering He witnesses. Could we bear seeing any more anyway? Increased awareness already overloads our limited bearing capacity, causing some to "tune out" and inducing still others to doubt God's purposes and capacity.

When trials of faith are no longer something we see happening to others but instead involve "me," it is more difficult! When a different configuration of challenges presents itself, for instance, even past experiences may not sustain us fully. Memory can surely help by keeping us meek and trusting in the face of what is new. The sobering indication "All these things shall give thee experience, and shall be for thy good" (D&C 122:7) tells us that while we are doctrinally rich, we are usually experience poor. God's plan is designed to correct the latter deficiency; one's soul shivers, however, as one contemplates the implications.

If we do not understand God's plan of salvation sufficiently, we will run the risk of misreading life's trials, whether these come to us or to our loved ones. Amid stress, if we do not understand the character of God and Jesus adequately—including their perfect love and omniscience—we may either doubt their love or question their tutoring wisdom.

Applying faith to daily life, therefore, amid the overall plan is not merely mental gymnastics involving abstract theology. Instead, faith becomes genuinely operative in our daily lives as we really begin to "liken" the doctrines "unto [our]selves" (1 Nephi 19:23). This effort to "liken" is part of being "anxiously engaged" in a risk-filled adventure.

If in God's plan of salvation there were not moral agency, risk, and uncertainty, resulting in the trying of our faith and patience, there would be no real growth or real happiness. Even God cannot try our patience without our having the relevant, clinical experiences in which impatience can so easily carry the day. How can we learn to "be of good cheer" without passing through situations of insecurity or anxiety?

Furthermore, in the isometrics of individual development God may try us where we are the weakest (see Ether 12:27). One understandably may wince while exploring the implications of that hard teaching!

Faith in the plan of salvation with its developmental dimensions makes allowance for the fact that so many undesirable things occur "in process of time." Exercising one's faith "in process of time" involves, as noted, the steady isometrics of pitting the old self against the new self. No wonder patience is also required in this, the most grinding and exhausting form of calisthenics.

Our youth are sometimes buffeted daily in Babylon beyond

what we who are older know. They need at least a rudimen-
tary understanding of the plan of salvation, especially in their
tender times of growing up. For them, in a moment of needed
response, the smile of one friend is like a standing ovation. A
compliment can part the curtain on their unappreciated possibilities. Unfortunately, however, our youth can almost be
terrorized by the disapproval of their peers. It is as if their
group's "thumbs down" were the equivalent of a Roman em-
peror dispatching with finality gladiators in the Colosseum.
Youth can be so easily devastated by cutting remarks, as if
such slights represented the irreversible verdict of the universe as to their worth. When so discouraged, the "eat, drink,
and be merry" philosophy can end up being alluring, especially if they do not understand God's plan, His love of them,
and what Jesus' atonement did for them, personally. The less
they feel of ultimate belonging, the more counterfeit forms of
belonging will appeal. Of course, ultimate belonging is not
just for teenagers. Lacking an understanding of the plan of
salvation, one may feel like a permanent resident in an airport
transit lounge with its busy, ever-changing, lonely crowd.

For all of us, much has been helpfully revealed about the
role of suffering and the purposes of individual chastisement
during this mortal proving (see Abraham 3:25; Mosiah 3:19;
23:21). These true doctrines can inform us and brace us. Ignorance of them, however, can squeeze out the hope that is
sorely needed to company with faith and charity.

The perception of one of Morris L. West's characters as to
the "tragedy of the human condition" is that man is "con-
ceived without consent" and "wrenched whimpering into an
alien universe."[2] Absent an understanding of God's plan of
salvation (which knowledge comes to mankind solely by revelation, not by induction, deduction, or observation), such
poignant feelings of lamentation may be expected. When
there is an accompanying sense of helplessness or a willingness to surrender to the temptations of the flesh, it should not
surprise us.

President Young reassured us as follows: "When you understand the Gospel plan, you will comprehend that it is the most reasonable way of dealing with the human family."[3] Yet "the most reasonable way" causes you and me to tremble when our trials seem unreasonable and unexpected.

One of faith's most trying experiences occurs when, after having given our loving help, we watch with feelings of helplessness the struggles of those we love. If their circumstance or suffering goes unrelieved, did we quit importuning the Lord too soon? If we had importuned a little longer, would things be different? How do we balance sincere importuning with submissively accepting what God has allotted to us? Only the Holy Ghost can give us such discernment and assurance. What a splendid gift is thus given to us!

In these tender and perplexing situations, each case is different. We sometimes genuinely don't know what to pray for "as we ought" (Romans 8:26). But the Spirit can tell us when our importuning has been sufficient and when it is time to accept what is allotted.

As to the simplicity and relevancy of the gospel, President Brigham Young observed:

> If you could see things as they are, you would know that the whole plan of salvation, and all the revelations ever given to man on the earth are as plain as would be the remarks of an Elder, were he to stand here and talk about our every day business. . . . You may now be inclined to say, "O, this is too simple and child-like, we wish to hear the mysteries of the kingdoms of the Gods who have existed from eternity, and of all the kingdoms in which they will dwell; we desire to have these things portrayed to our understandings." Allow me to inform you that you are in the midst of it all now.[4]

Having faith in the plan of salvation makes all the difference in how we see our personal situation amid what others call the human predicament. The Apostle Paul understood the plan, and his faith was such "that all things work together for good to them that love God" (Romans 8:28). Nephi, though momentarily perplexed, similarly observed: "I know that [God] loveth his children; nevertheless, I do not know the meaning of all things" (1 Nephi 11:17).

We know, for example, that some either enter into this life with, or subsequently acquire, significant and disabling limitations to their capacity to function fully. The meaning of such situations is not quickly apparent in all such instances. Nevertheless, even with their severe limitations some of these individuals are so valiant. They do so much with so little! One senses, at times, that they press almost eagerly against those limitations, as if they were trying to "get out."

One day, when we have a fulness of facts, we will see yet another application of the parable of the talents as pertains to these individuals who do so much with so little. Surely in God's perfect love and mercy, those who have been thus valiant will hear their own deserved version of, "Well done, thou good and faithful servant." If, further, it also turns out that there was a premortal agreement by them to accept their limitations, so much more reason to rejoice and to admire them. Meanwhile, their response to their limitations should concern us less than how we respond to these special individuals.

Having faith in the Father's macro plan of salvation includes making allowance for His micro plans as well, just as having faith in His character encourages us to become more like Him and His Son, Jesus Christ. Emulation becomes the highest form of adoration.

However, what if God had His ego only *mostly* under control? Or where would we be if, instead of focusing on bringing "to pass the immortality and eternal life of man," God were distracted by self-centeredness? In fact, God has described what His work is, and does nothing save it be for the benefit of man (see Moses 1:39; 2 Nephi 26:24). Where would we be, too, if our Father in Heaven experienced people fatigue and we were merely His annoying posterity who kept Him from doing what He really wanted to do? Or where would we be if God became bored with the whole process?

As life presses upon us with both goodness and relentless-ness, we must pace ourselves and recognize the limitations that go with our "strength and means" (D&C 10:4). Yes, we should do things in "wisdom and order" (Mosiah 4:27). Granted, there are times when we need respite and renewal, our equivalent of going to "a desert place . . . privately" (Mark 6:32). But though we can acknowledge this, why wouldn't a loving Father, full of joy, want all His children to have *all* that He has and therefore provide the growth conditions that could make this possible? How would we feel, later on, if we learned that He had not so striven in behalf of His children, earnestly wanting His children to receive "all that [He] hath"? (See D&C 84:38.) No wonder His efforts in our behalf are so unceasing.

God's comprehensive plan of salvation is the means by which He achieves all of His purposes.

Is it any wonder, then, if, in His plan, our "faith and pa-tience" are regularly tried? (See Mosiah 23:21.) Paul confirms that those who "inherit the promises" are those who have tri-umphed "through faith and patience" (Hebrews 6:12). Abra-ham "obtained the promise," but only "after he had patiently endured" (Hebrews 6:15). Long-suffering, endurance, and pa-tience are designed to be constant companions, as are faith, hope, and charity.

While a person is thinking his way through his particular hesitations or reservations about faith, he might ask, "Does God really know what I am passing through?" The answer is "Yes!" He knows! He also *knew*—through His foreknowledge. We worship an omniscient Father—a stunning characteristic of God which we forget at the peril of our perspective. Hence understanding the implications of key doctrines is part of fur-ther developing one's faith.

One may ask, With all else God has to do, does He really

care about me or mine? Yes! He is a perfect Father, with attributes of perfect love and mercy. He is not only fully aware, but He cares. He knows, too, how good and conscientious parents can sometimes "take" more themselves than they can watch their children "take." But since He would not take away the cup from His Only Begotten and "Beloved Son" in Gethsemane and Calvary, He will not always intervene for us, either, as we might sincerely desire in the life crises of our children.

Does God already know the outcome of that through which I am passing? Yes! And He has taken that outcome, foreknown to Him, into account along with all other outcomes. In the Prophet Joseph Smith's words, God "has made ample provision,"[5] so that the purposes in His plan of salvation will be achieved—including our part within that plan, if we are faithful.

The inability to believe in the foreknowledge of the Father and Jesus and in their perfect love perhaps accounts for many failures of faith. As some encounter life's proving purposes, resentment of the challenges may cause a misunderstanding of God's plan. To those of little faith, His nonintervention is mistakenly taken to mean God either isn't there or doesn't care.

Mormon assured us, however, that Christ "advocateth the cause of the children of men" (Moroni 7:28). Other "good causes" pale by comparison. Angels help to "call men unto repentance . . . by declaring the word of Christ unto the chosen vessels of the Lord, that they may bear testimony of him. And by so doing, the Lord God prepareth the way that the residue[6] of men may have faith in Christ, that the Holy Ghost may have place in their hearts . . . ; and after this manner bringeth to pass the Father, the covenants which he hath made unto the children of men." (Moroni 7:31–32.) Therefore, those who discount angels and angelically delivered truths underestimate God's capacity to achieve His purposes for man "in [his] own way" (D&C 104:16).

The "most believing," however, are truly "alive in Christ," though in a dying world. These few have "hope through the atonement of Christ and the power of His resurrection." They "have faith in Christ because of [their] meekness." (Moroni 7:39, 41.) Just as important, they are filled with charity and "faith unfeigned" (see 2 Corinthians 6:6). Even for high-achieving individuals, however, personal development occurs "in process of time."

This whole, glorious dispensation of the fulness of times began with the simple act of faith by a very young man who had read a verse about faith written centuries before by faithful James. Young Joseph had a genuine desire to know which Church to join. He "gave place" (see Alma 32:28) in his schedule and his life and found a place to pray vocally, thereby exercising his faith. Then the mighty restoration began, with its precious revelations; and none was more needed than those about the plan of salvation.

No sooner do we begin to display a little faith, however, than that faith is tried—just as happened in the Sacred Grove.

Yet without the trials which come even to early faith, greater things cannot subsequently be revealed to us. Only after our faith is tried can we receive the witness which is subsequently needed to sustain us (see Ether 12:6).

Even so, amid life's tests we may still sometimes wonder, if only inwardly, "Why me? Why this? Why now?" The remedy, Brigham Young indicated, is for "the Spirit of revelation [to] be in each and every individual, to know the plan of salvation and keep in the path that leads them to the presence of God."[7] There can be no such personal revelation, however, without our first developing personal faith in God's patterns of divine disclosure.

Let it be said, however, that not only does God have a plan but so also does the adversary. President Young assured us that "the Lord Jesus Christ works upon a plan of eternal increase, of wisdom, intelligence, honor, excellence, power, glory, might, and dominion, and the attributes that fill eternity. What principle does the devil work upon? It is to destroy, dissolve, decompose, and tear in pieces."[8] This destruction includes marriages, friendships, faith, self-esteem, and purposeful living in all its dimensions.

Why is it so hard, then, especially if we know and understand these things? One major reason is the impact of the flesh (see chapter 6). We also live in the dimension of time which, by its very nature, creates vexing suspense for us. Life is so designed that we use our moral agency by choosing for ourselves daily. This steady stream of our responses forms a cumulative record out of which we will later be judged. This same plan, a framework for life, ensures that we are to overcome by faith, not by perfect knowledge.

One of the purposes of the Father's plan of salvation is that "all these things shall give thee experience, and shall be for thy good" (D&C 122:7). This means that we are proffered the necessary experience in enduring, choosing, and learning from various outcomes. In this way we get to know ourselves, our strengths and our weaknesses. If meek, we get experience in developing empathy, not only for those close to us but for others as well who are struggling to make it through this second estate successfully.

Since the natural man is too attached to his possessions anyway, the plan requires that we must have experience in giving possessions away—in sharing and even losing them—in order to give us experience with the principle of sacrifice without worrying about getting credit or receiving recognition as we worship Him who made the "great and last sacrifice" (Alma 34:10).

Since the natural man is also too selfish and too caught up with himself, there must be experiences which are empathy enhancing.

Since the natural man is likewise too impatient, there must be experiences to teach patience.

Since the natural man is inclined to hold back his talents, his time, or his possessions, there will also be enhancing experiences to teach us, if we will, the need to let our wills be swallowed up in the will of the Father.

Since the natural man is too proud, there will be meek-ness-enhancing experiences.

Despite our need for these experiences, we mortals are free to choose for ourselves whether to use for our good the experiences through which we pass. In his plan, God "permits" many things of which He clearly does not approve. Brigham Young taught: "The inquiry may rise, 'Does the Lord reign upon the earth?' We could answer, 'Yes; for it is his earth, and he controlleth according to his pleasure, and it will yet be devoted to those who serve him. But, in consequence of the agency that is given to the intelligent children of our Father and God, it is contrary to his laws, government, and character for him to dictate us in our actions any further than we prefer.'"[9]

President Joseph F. Smith said: "Many things occur in the world in which it seems very difficult for most of us to find a solid reason for the acknowledgment of the hand of the Lord. I have come to the belief that the only reason I have been able to discover by which we should acknowledge the hand of God in some occurrences is the fact that the thing which has occurred has been permitted of the Lord."[10]

Faithful and tried John Taylor candidly said we need to have faith in the plan, even when we do not have all the explanatory divine data: "I do not know why Jesus should leave his Father's throne and be offered up a sacrifice for the sin of the world, and why mankind have to be put through such an ordeal as they have to pass through on this earth; we reason upon this, and the Scriptures say that it is because man cannot be made perfect only through suffering. We might ask why could not mankind be saved in another way? why could not salvation be wrought out without suffering? *I receive it in my faith that this is the only way,* and I rejoice that we have a Savior who had the goodness to come forth and redeem us."[11]

Real storm fronts do pass turbulently through our lives, but they do not last forever. We can learn the important difference between passing, local cloud cover, and general darkness.

43

We can "hold out," if we but hold on by maintaining our perspective. But while we are in the midst of "all these things," the very experiences which can be for our long-term good, the anguish is real. We may feel, for instance, that some trials are simply more than we can bear. Yet, if we have faith in God's character as an all-knowing and all-loving Father, we understand that in His plan He will not give us more than we can bear. (See 1 Corinthians 10:13; D&C 50:40.)

The role of moral agency in God's plan of salvation is crucial. Since things have a way of going awry whenever we mortals misuse our agency, there is great need for us to develop our own capacity to extend long-suffering and mercy towards others, even when their mistakes adversely affect us. The injunction of forgiving "seventy times seven" not only instructs us but also implies much about the frequency of mortal errors, thus reinforcing the counsel for us to be long-suffering.

Just as God provided in His plan a Savior for mankind, He has not left mankind alone in other ways. From time to time in human history He has given Apostles and prophets for the "edifying" of the Church and to bless all who would pay heed to them (see Ephesians 4:11–14). *Edifying* means "building up," with all that implies. The Church of Jesus Christ of Latter-day Saints seeks to promote the edifying numerical and spiritual growth of its membership. No wonder the Joseph Smith Translation of the familiar Matthew 6:33 stresses that we are to seek *first* to "build up" the kingdom of God and to "establish" His righteousness. Then "all these things shall be added unto you." (JST, Matthew 6:38.) The building up of individuals by helping them to establish righteousness in their lives is at the core of Heavenly Father's purposes in restoring His Church.

Lest we be too intimidated about the plan of salvation's eventual emphasis on our becoming perfect, as the Father and Jesus are, it is well to keep in mind that the word *perfect* emphasizes that one can become "finished" and "fully developed" (see Matthew 5:48; 3 Nephi 12:48; 27:27; Ephesians

4:13). It thus emphasizes the "completeness" and wholeness essential to full happiness, including, of course, the glorious resurrection and joyous exaltation. However, instead of resulting in a democratic sameness among all resurrected people in each and every respect, God's plan clearly accepts that there will be variations of attainment. These will reflect how well we lived in mortality and to what extent we developed our individual possibilities.

Enduring affliction is certainly part of enduring to the end, but the word *enduring* also means to last, to continue, and to remain (see 2 Nephi 33:9). This emphasis on staying the course appears at so many points in the scriptures (for examples, see D&C 20:29; 2 Nephi 9:24). We could scarcely become "finished" or "completed" if we did not finish and complete all of life's assigned course!

Since the plan of salvation is aimed at our individual spiritual development, it is well for us to take account of life's high-risk situations. One tremendous risk is possessing power, though this is a circumstance for which many crave (see D&C 121:34–46). There is currently much fascination with empowerment but very little interest in the everlasting significance of the attribute of meekness, which was so perfectly embodied in the character of Jesus, our great Exemplar.

President Abraham Lincoln, a student of human nature, knew firsthand of the interplay of political power and purpose. He wrote eloquently of the persistent human strivings for power and for glory, especially among the talented:

This field of glory is harvested, and the crop is already appropriated. But new reapers will arise, and they, too, will seek a field. It is to deny, what the history of the world tells us is true, to suppose that men of ambition and talents will not continue to spring up amongst us. . . . Towering genius disdains a beaten path. It seeks regions hitherto unexplored. It sees no distinction in adding story to story, upon the monuments of fame, erected to the memory of others. It denies that it is glory enough to serve under any chief. It scorns to tread in the footsteps of any predecessor, however illustrious. It thirsts and burns for distinction; and, if possible, it will have it, whether at the expense of emancipating slaves, or enslaving freemen.[12]

Another high risk while we pass through the second estate of the plan of salvation is the human tendency to assume one has intellectual self-sufficiency and can disregard divine revelation. Skepticism abounds about the very process of revelation. Ironically, it is by revelation that we know anything at all about the plan of salvation! One could stare at the stars a long time, even appreciatively and with the radio telescope, without ever discovering God's purposes for the universe.

The denial of revelation has been and is expressed variously:

And now behold, I, Sherem, declare unto you that . . . no man knoweth of such things; for he cannot tell of things to come (Jacob 7:7).

Why do ye look for a Christ? For no man can know of anything which is to come.

How do ye know of their surety? Behold, ye cannot know of things which ye do not see; therefore ye cannot know that there shall be a Christ. (Alma 30:13, 15.)

Some, though sincere, nevertheless discount revelation, simply because they cannot really accept that God exists, as Joseph Smith taught, in "an eternal now" with the past, the present, and the future before him.[13] But having faith in the Father's plan of salvation is tied to having faith in this vital dimension of His character and capacity.

God's plan of salvation features His invitation, "Come home!" Our Father's invitation was thus accompanied by the restoration of all the implementing priesthood keys, authority, ordinances, and doctrines. It truly was a "marvelous work and a wonder"—wording denoting something "extraordinary"—but it is also clearly something "hard to understand" (see Isaiah 29:14).

With the Restoration came a clear understanding of our true identity and a sense of everlasting community. We know who we really are and where our "home" really is. Hence life, when properly lived, is really a journey "back home." In this narrow sense we are like the prodigal son. As we come to ourselves, we too will say with determination, "I will arise and go to my father" (Luke 15:18).

The Prophet Joseph Smith learned so much about the overall plan of happiness throughout the extended process of the Lord's restoring of the holy apostleship, the holy priesthood, the holy endowment, the holy sealing power, and so forth. Yet young Joseph, whose impact would become global, merely went into the Sacred Grove to find out which local church he should join. How generous God is!

The Father's plan, then, was set up to bring us all the way "home." Upon entering the third estate, however, we will never know the welcoming embrace of the celestial gate's keeper if in this second estate we embrace the things of the world (see 2 Nephi 9:41; Mormon 5:11; 6:17).

Of course, some can be content with being numbered among the "honorable" terrestrials (D&C 76:75). Yet each of us has been invited to become "the man [or woman] of Christ" (see Hebrews 12:9; Helaman 3:29; 3 Nephi 27:27; D&C 76:24).

Hence no temporary designation and no other way of being known here on earth should take precedence. Having faith in the plan of salvation includes steadfastly refusing to be diverted from our true identities and responsibilities. In the brief season of our existence on earth we may serve as plumber, professor, farmer, physician, mechanic, bookkeeper, or teacher. These are useful activities and honorable designations; but a temporary vocation is not reflective of our true identities. Matthew was a tax collector, Luke a physician, and Peter a fisherman. In a salvational sense, "So what!"

Because God knows our true identities, He loves us too much to let us be content with what we have achieved spiritually up to now. He is a perfect Father who knows what we have the power to become, and He has His special ways of being lovingly insistent.

Magnifying our callings signifies our willingness to be further tutored and trained—all in order to become the "man [or woman] of Christ." The more we become like Jesus, the more useful we are to Him and the more prepared to live with Him.

Even the various offices and Church callings we hold should not be seen as limitations but as intrinsic invitations to facilitate our going home, having been "added upon" (see Abraham 3:26).

To magnify one's calling means seeing "with the eye of faith" the enlarged and detailed possibilities of service to one's family, flock, friends, and others. After all, the same power of God that brought into existence "worlds without number" (Moses 1:33) can surely watch over our little universes of individual experience!

Of the great invitation we have received to "come home," the Prophet Joseph Smith declared, "If you wish to go where God is, you must be like God, or possess the principles which God possesses."[14] King Benjamin was specific in saying that if one wishes to become a saint, he must become "as a child, submissive, meek, humble, patient, full of love, willing to submit to all things which the Lord seeth fit to inflict upon him, even as a child doth submit to his father" (Mosiah 3:19).

The more one sees of life, the more one understands why there is such a scriptural stress on submissiveness and meekness. The dangers flowing from an excess of ego are real and constant. Would that we first placed an ego-filtering screen over all our thoughts, words, and actions *before* they hurt others or embarrassed us. If we are steadily becoming more and more the man or woman of Christ, the filtering mesh in that ego screen will become finer; fewer things will slip through to harm.

Some questions may help us to "audit" how much operative faith we have in the Father's plan of salvation.

- How perceptibly are we developing the Christlike qualities enumerated by King Benjamin?
- What will our sons, daughters, grandsons, and granddaughters learn from us about gospel doctrines? Or will we depend entirely upon Church classrooms to teach our children?
- Does our understanding of the plan of salvation help us to handle disappointments in life? Can we partake of our tiny, bitter cups without becoming bitter?
- How often do we render quiet, Christian service? A lack of sufficient love for others constitutes a major failure for which no other successes can ever fully compensate.

How consistently do we show love and respect for our family members? for women? There is no real manhood without real respect for womanhood. No man can be exalted who demeans women. Surely no man who is brutal, harsh, or disrespectful to a wife or mother or children or to any woman is worthy of his priesthood! Since our sons and grandsons will treat women much as we men now do, what generational proclivities are we building?

Likewise, our daughters and granddaughters will regard men much as their mothers do.

One seldom-mentioned reason for keeping the commandments is that we then become genuinely happier with ourselves. Otherwise, if unhappy with ourselves, the grim tendency is to pass our misery on, or at least to allow it to cloud and even diminish the lives of others who must put up with us. Our happiness is the intent of God's plan of happiness.

The more we come to understand the plan of happiness, the more we come to understand how incomplete and unfinished we were in our first estate and how much we needed this difficult mortal experience. We finally realize that there is no other way. Remembering this reality helps, especially when the only way is so difficult and discouraging at times and when we experience sadness as participants in the great plan of happiness.

We can take heart and rejoice when we see the divine virtues well developed in our fellow servants. It gives the rest of us hope and encouragement. "You can do it!" is best received from someone who has done it. We understand, therefore, that sometimes the less heralded but highly developed individuals are "no less serviceable" (Alma 48:19) in the cause of God than those who may be much more in the spotlight.

The best thing we can do is to be in the serious process of becoming the men and women of Christ. If we are moving in the direction of becoming more loving, meek, humble, patient, long-suffering, kind, and gentle, then all those we lead will be safe with us; we will lead our flocks as Christ leads the Church (see Ephesians 5:23).

The cardinal virtues are always the ones most needed for living in close, mortal quarters, anyway. It is in close quarters that we experience and endure each other's imperfections. This is one reason why patience and forgiveness are such cardinal virtues, especially in families.

With regard to our small world of families and flocks, how wonderful it would be if it could be correctly said of each of us what is correctly said of our Father: that He "doeth not anything save it be for the benefit of the world"! (2 Nephi 26:24.) Would that we'd not do "anything save it be for the benefit" of our family, friends, and flocks.

As we move along the pathway on the journey back home, it is only fair to acknowledge that, even with all its resultant blessings, faithfulness will bring some added challenges. It seems God is always stretching most those who meekly serve Him. At times His best pupils experience the most rigorous and continuous courses. Eventually, each who proves to be a man or woman of Christ will thereby become a distinguished alumnus of life's school of affliction, graduating with honors. This is a wintry doctrine, but a true one. And complying with each wintry doctrine brings its own summer-like set of rewards.

Knowing of God's plan, we should beware of any group that requires us to alienate ourselves from God in order to belong. We should be careful, too, of any rites of social passage if these are the very passages that lead down to the gulf of misery and woe (see Helaman 3:29; 5:12).

Finally, consider how long ago some were actually called: "And this is the manner after which they were ordained—being called and prepared *from the foundation of the world* according to the foreknowledge of God, on account of their exceeding faith and good works" (Alma 13:3, italics added).

Foreordinations for men and foredesignations for women happened a long, long time ago. Let us be true to those anticipations by striving to journey "home" complete with our families. Jesus has gone ahead to prepare a place for us. Meanwhile, however, there may be some dark days immediately ahead, but with brighter days eventually ahead.

In 480 B.C. a small Greek force under the Spartan king Leonidas courageously held a mountain pass for three days at a place called Thermopylae against overwhelming numbers of the enemy. When someone commented that the Persian army was so huge that their arrows blocked out the sun, one of the defenders replied: "So much the better. We shall fight in the shade!"[15]

In the life of each of us there is intermittent shade brought by passing cloud cover. It takes operative faith in the Father's plan to survive, whether in the shade or under the scorching, secular sun. Both discouraging shade and the heat of the sun bring out our weaknesses. By relying on faith, we repent and improve in honest recognition of those inadequacies. Otherwise—without faith—why bother to change?

In this life, clearly we "walk by faith" rather than by perfect knowledge (2 Corinthians 5:7). The plan ensures that our perspective is intentionally limited. Elder Charles W. Penrose perceptively instructed:

The knowledge of our former state has fled from us. . . . and the veil is drawn between us and our former habitation. This is for our trial. If we could see the things of eternity, and comprehend ourselves as we are; if we could penetrate the mists and clouds that shut out eternal realities from our gaze, the fleeting things of time would be no trial to us, and one of the great objects of our earthly probation or testing would be lost. But the past has gone from our memory, the future is shut out from our vision and we are living here in time, to learn little by little, line upon line, precept upon precept. Here in the darkness, in the sorrow, in the trial, in the pain, in the adversity, we have to learn what is right and distinguish it from what is wrong, and lay hold of right and truth and learn to live it. . . . If we have any evil propensities . . . we have to grapple with them and overcome them. Each individual must find out his own nature, and what there is in it that is wrong, and bring it into subjection to the will and righteousness of God.[16]

In the rigorous second estate, the inherent journey of self-discovery is best made. Wilford Woodruff confirmed: "There is a vail between man and eternal things; if that vail was taken away and we were able to see eternal things as they are before the Lord, no man would be tried with regard to gold, silver or this world's goods . . . and this [vail is there] for a wise and proper purpose in the Lord our God, to prove whether the children of men will abide in his law or not in the situation in which they are placed here."[17]

One day, however, full perspective will be ours, as President Brigham Young declared:

> We talk about our trials and troubles here in this life: but suppose that you could see yourselves thousands and millions of years after you have proved faithful to your religion during the few short years in this time, and have obtained eternal salvation and a crown of glory in the presence of God; then look back upon your lives here, and see the losses, crosses, and disappointments, the sorrows . . . you would be constrained to exclaim, "But what of all that? Those things were but for a moment, and we are now here."[18]

Even though we are presently shorn of perspective, if we have faith we can face the darkness and life's fiery trials.

Shadrach, Meshach, and Abed-nego, three valiant young men, knew that God could easily rescue them from the fiery furnace if He so chose. "But if not" they said, they would believe in and trust Him anyway! (See Daniel 3:18.) Since death comes to all of us, the tersely expressed faith of two Book of Mormon prophets too is worthy of emulation. So far as the specific timing of their own deaths was concerned, they said, if they could but do their duty, "it matters not." (See Mosiah 13:9; Ether 15:34.)

It should be the same with us. Blessings are given to some who are sick and they are healed, some quickly and some slowly. But some are not healed. Moreover, some wrenching conditions provide sharp, persistent thorns in the flesh which are to be endured, not removed (see 2 Corinthians 12:7).

President Lorenzo Snow, speaking of the *universal* plan of salvation with its *personal* trials, once quoted some sobering and confirming lines of poetry:

> All who journey soon or late,
> Must come within the garden gate,
> And kneel alone in darkness there,
> And battle hard, yet not despair.[19]

Successfully meeting our trials, therefore, shows we have faith in the Father's plan of salvation. Besides, being too comfortable here would only produce a later discomfort, for, as President Woodruff counseled, "if we had no trials we should hardly feel at home in the other world in the company of the Prophets and Apostles who were sawn asunder, crucified, etc., for the word of God and testimony of Jesus Christ."[20]

Having faith in the Father's plan of salvation includes allowing for that suffering, including the vexations growing out of some interpersonal relationships. Of these vexations, John Taylor observed: "Many of us are tried and tempted, and we get harsh and hard feelings against one another. And it reminds me of your teams when going down hill with a heavy load. When the load begins to crowd on to the horses, you will frequently see one snap at his mate, and the other will prick up his ears and snap back again. And why? A little while before, perhaps, and they were playing with each other. Because the load crowds on them. Well, when the load begins to crowd, do not snap at your brethren, but let them feel that you are their friends, and pull together."[21]

If we now have full faith in the Father's plan of salvation, one day we will look back with fulness of fact and acknowledge God's perfect justice and mercy (see Mosiah 27:31; Alma 12:15).

Mercifully, the Restoration scriptures came to inspire, inform, and bolster us. God knew we urgently needed these added, precious pages of holy writ with their "convincing" content. We could not do His work in this last and full dispensation without them.

CHAPTER

4

Faith in the
Book of Mormon

A great deal of what we know about Jesus' role, atonement, and character and about the Father's plan of salvation comes to us from the precious Restoration scriptures. A major source is the Book of Mormon with its "convincing," Christ-centered content. The Book of Mormon, Another Testament of Jesus Christ, was also provided by the Lord as a tangible, enduring witness to the prophetic mission of Joseph Smith.

The coming forth of the Book of Mormon preceded all the other Restoration scriptures in providing refreshing, renewing, and convincing evidence about Jesus and about God's plan of salvation. Indeed, the substance of the Restoration scriptures responds to life's largest and most troubling issues.

Today's appreciative readers of the Book of Mormon will understand quickly the reverence for God's "word" as was displayed in ancient Israel. When the prophet Ezra read and taught the law of Moses to his people at the feast of tabernacles, he stood upon an elevated pulpit "in the sight of all the people," and "opened the book," and reverently "all the people stood up." They were taught to "understand the reading," and "all the people wept when they heard the words of the law." (See Nehemiah 8:2–9.) The Book of Mormon surely deserves equivalent reverence and respect, not to be "treated lightly" (see D&C 84:54).

A modern prophet, another Ezra (President Ezra Taft Benson), has stressed both how valuable the Book of Mormon is and our obligation to read it regularly. "There are three ways in which the Book of Mormon is the keystone of our religion. It is the keystone in our witness of Christ. It is the keystone of our doctrine. It is the keystone of testimony."[1]

Even so, divinely directed enterprises, which are rightly described as marvelous and wondrous, scarcely lend themselves to superficial scrutiny or to casual explanations. Hence, if such enterprises are approached without meekness and without a sense of spiritual proportion, wondrous things they contain can be so easily trivialized by one's "looking beyond the mark." Take, for example, Jesus' miracle of the loaves (see Matthew 14:15–21; 15:32–38). We do not know just how such a miracle was actually performed. Did the few loaves subdivide? Or did the additional loaves (from which there were even twelve basketfuls left over) fall like manna from heaven? Did the remarkable multiplication or replenishment occur during Jesus' prayer or during distribution? It was the miracle showing Jesus' divinity that really mattered, not the unrevealed details of the process by which it occurred.

It is much the same with the coming forth and translation of the Book of Mormon. "For in that day, for my sake shall the Father work a work, which shall be a great and a marvelous work among them; and there shall be among them those who will not believe it, although a man shall declare it unto them" (3 Nephi 21:9).

The Restoration cannot be "a marvelous work and a wonder" without at the same time being seen by some as unlikely, unusual, and unexpected. As the Lord prepares to "prune [his] vineyard for the last time," He will, He says, "bring to pass my strange act, that I may pour out my Spirit upon all flesh" (D&C 95:4). The very word *strange* connotes something unfamiliar. Certainly the Restoration, especially as viewed by a secular society, qualifies as unfamiliar and unusual: "That wise men and rulers may hear and know that which they have never considered; that I may proceed to bring to pass my act, my strange act, and perform my work, my strange work, that men may discern between the righteous and the wicked, saith your God" (D&C 101:94–95; see also Isaiah 28:21).

Some, if meek, will actually "hear and know that which they have never considered" (D&C 101:94). But the Lord told Joseph Smith that some would not believe even if they saw "all these things which I have committed unto you" (D&C 5:7).

Many prophets and writers contributed to the Book of Mormon, in which various records were merged and edited.[2]

Mormon and all the other writers did not have access to today's user-friendly word processors. Instead, they made engravings on metal plates. It was not easy. Jacob wrote: "I, Jacob, . . . cannot write but a little of my words, because of the difficulty of engraving our words upon plates" (Jacob 4:1).

Various descriptive phrases noted the constraints. Omni wrote "somewhat upon these plates" (Omni 1:1). Likewise, Mormon "did forebear to make a full account" (Mormon 2:18). Nephi told Jacob to select things which were "most precious," engraving "the heads" of only that "which was great" "upon these plates." (Jacob 1:2, 4.) Since not everything could be covered, Nephi wrote about "the things of [his] soul" (2 Nephi 4:15).

Some "custodians" of the ancient plates essentially passed the plates along. Amaron, for instance, wrote in a single day the several lines he added (see Omni 1:4–9). Abinadom was equally terse: "I know of no revelation save that which has been written, neither prophecy; wherefore, that which is sufficient is written. And I make an end." (Omni 1:11.) However, each did his duty, caring for the sacred records and then passing the plates along. We are in debt to these individuals too.

Periodically, some had to smelt ore: "And it came to pass that the Lord commanded me, wherefore I did make plates of ore that I might engraven upon them the record of my people" (1 Nephi 19:1).

Late in the process, Moroni ran out not only of plates but even of ore. He also ran out of family, enduring aching, personal loneliness as he cared for the sacred records. "Behold, my father hath made this record, and he hath written the intent thereof. And behold, I would write it also if I had room upon the plates, but I have not; and ore I have none, for I am alone. My father hath been slain in battle, and all my kinsfolk, and I have not friends nor whither to go; and how long the Lord will suffer that I may live I know not." (Mormon 8:5.)

Moroni not only contributed to the record his own content but also transported the heavy plates over undisclosed miles.

It is estimated that from a first edition of 5,000 copies of the Book of Mormon in 1830 on through 1992, nearly 65,000,000 copies have been sold, including nearly 5,000,000 copies in 1992.

Furthermore, the Book of Mormon's influence will continue to grow. "Wherefore, these things shall go from generation to generation as long as the earth shall stand; and they shall go according to the will and pleasure of God; and the nations who shall possess them shall be judged of them according to the words which are written" (2 Nephi 25:22). Hence the Book of Mormon's best days still lie ahead.

There are yet other foretelling words, saying that "the day cometh that the words of the book which were sealed shall be read upon the house tops" (2 Nephi 27:11). And why not, in consideration of something which is a "marvellous work and a wonder"? (Isaiah 29:14.)

Joseph Smith worked by the "gift" and "power of God" amid numerous interruptions, bitter persecutions, and the "most strenuous exertions" of others to steal the actual plates from him (Book of Mormon title page; D&C 1:29; 135:3; Joseph Smith—History 1:60).

Joseph's was not the tranquil life of a scholar in some sheltered sanctuary, where he could work at his uninterrupted leisure. Chores had to be done. His family had to be cared for. Joseph was so conscientious that the Lord counseled him: "Do not run faster or labor more than you have strength and means provided to enable you to translate; but be diligent unto the end" (D&C 10:4).

Why was it so vital to have another book of scripture join the Bible in our age? Some have called our current period in human history the post-Christian world, as if Christianity were largely over and done with. Hence, in that slackening of faith, the Christ-centered nature of the Restoration message is highly relevant.

While Joseph Smith's own time and location was one of religious fervor among Christian sects—"Lo, here! . . . Lo, there!" (Joseph Smith—History 1:5)—ours is a skeptical world. In nations once regarded as basically Christian, many now are unsure or disbelieving about Jesus.

The Restoration is so relevant and so timely. After all, the Book of Mormon's stated purpose is for "the convincing of the Jew and Gentile that Jesus is the Christ" (title page), making it such a gift to the entire human family! "And it shall come to pass, that if the Gentiles shall hearken unto the Lamb of God in that day that he shall *manifest himself unto them in word,* and also in power, in very deed, unto the taking away of their stumbling blocks" (1 Nephi 14:1, italics added).

Specific faith does need to be increased in the world, and this requires the removal of certain stumbling blocks. Modern music, movies, and books reflect a sense of growing despair and disbelief. For example, one philosopher's summary of a nineteenth-century view of the universe was that life is "of profound unimportance . . . a 'mere eddy in the primeval slime.'"[3] Yet mankind is actually at the center of God's work.

In fact, Nephi tells us that God "doeth not anything save it be for the benefit of the world" (2 Nephi 26:24). The knowledge concerning God's plan of salvation, repeatedly and carefully set forth in the Book of Mormon, can counter the hopelessness and despair as some lament the human predicament.

No wonder the Lord told Joseph Smith that the Restoration came to "increase [faith] in the earth"! (D&C 1:21.)

Some partial believers in God question whether or not God can bring His purposes to fulfillment. In the Book of Mormon the Lord assures us, bluntly, two times in two verses, "I will show unto the children of men that I am able to do mine own work" (see 2 Nephi 27:20–21).

In the book's translation, Emma Smith was one of Joseph's early scribes amid difficult circumstances. One later episode illustrates Emma's dedication amid hardship.

> Emma Smith made her departure from Far West, Missouri, with a group of Saints on 7 February 1839. Her husband still languished in a "lonesome prison" in Liberty, Missouri. . . . Emma finally arrived at the western shore of the frozen Mississippi River. Somewhat fearful of the thin ice, she separated her two horses and walked apart with the two-and-one-half-year-old Frederick and eight-month-old Alexander in her arms. Julia held securely to her skirt on one side and positioned young Joseph on the other side to begin the walk across the river.
>
> Emma also carried Joseph's manuscripts of his Bible translation in heavy bags, along with her husband's other personal papers fastened securely to her waist. She then walked across the frozen river to safety in Illinois.[4]

We owe Emma for her part in the Restoration!

Martin Harris was also an early scribe; and he helped by generously funding the first printing of the Book of Mormon, an act which cost him much ridicule as well as considerable financial resources.

Oliver Cowdery was the devoted, able, and major scribe. But more about him later.

Hyrum Smith also gave the Prophet Joseph vital support and encouragement, including helping with the printer's manuscript at the press. Imagine what it would have been like if, in addition to all else he suffered, Joseph had had constant family ridicule and persecution.

E. B. Grandin printed the first edition of the Book of Mormon. Out of perceived necessity, Grandin's composition man, John H. Gilbert, provided some needed paragraphing and punctuating.[5] Referring to the manuscript, Gilbert wrote, "Every chapter, if I remember correctly, was one solid paragraph, without a punctuation mark, from beginning to end."[6] The first edition of the Book of Mormon reflects almost solid blocks of print. Though the printer's manuscript actually contained some punctuation and a few paragraph marks, the few surviving portions of the original manuscript contain no punctuation.

The 1837 and 1840 editions contain corrections, most of which were minor grammatical changes and clarifications.[7] The 1840 edition corrected some scribal errors, such as were made in copying the printer's manuscript from the original.

Of course it was the Book of Mormon's scriptural substance and doctrinal richness that really mattered, not its mortal punctuation or even its spelling.

Given its unique importance, it is not surprising that ever since the Book of Mormon was published in 1830 disbelievers and detractors have preferred *any* explanation of its coming forth to the real one! This disdain was foreseen by the Lord, who consoled Joseph: "Behold, if they will not believe my words, they would not believe you, my servant Joseph, if it were possible that you should show them all these things which I have committed unto you" (D&C 5:7).

Apparently, even if skeptics had been shown the Urim and Thummim and the plates, it would not have convinced them. Besides, reformed Egyptian is a language "none other people knoweth" (see Mormon 9:32, 34).

One early enemy of the Church, E. D. Howe, mistakenly

supposed that the author of the Book of Mormon was the Reverend Solomon Spaulding, who died in 1816, fourteen years before the Book of Mormon was published. The Spaulding "explanation" once caused such a needless stir! Spaulding's writings lack doctrinal and spiritual substance, though a few see very scattered similarities in "story lines."

The Solomon Spaulding manuscript is a fictional story about a group of Romans who, while sailing to England early in the fourth century A.D., were blown off course and landed in northeastern America. One of them kept a record of their experiences among the eastern and midwestern Indian tribes. It is amusing to compare samples such as the following with the Book of Mormon:

> The Reader will recollect that Elseon & his friends left Moonrod & his friends in a very pleasant mood without the least suspicion that Lamesa & her friend had deserted them. When they had arived at the vilage, what was their surprise when they found Lamesa & her friend were not in company— nor had any one any recollections of her being in company— after they had stoped to take their leave of Elseon. Moonrod & the other Gentlemen immediately rode back with the greatest speed to the place where they had halted, & not finding any traces of Lamesa, the conclusion was then certain that she had prefer the company of the young Prince & was on her way to Kentuck—Pursuit would be in vain, their only alternative was to hasten back & carry the doleful intelligence to the Emperor.[8]

Others said Sidney Rigdon (who first met Joseph several months after the Book of Mormon was published) authored the Book of Mormon, something Brother Rigdon never claimed.

In more recent years, another "explanation" has been advanced: Joseph Smith supposedly took his main ideas, say these critics, from the writings of one Ethan Smith, who wrote a book called *View of the Hebrews*, though there is no evidence that the Prophet ever knew anything about this book. But what is much more important, with regard to the purposes, style, and substance of the two books, comparing Ethan Smith's book *View of the Hebrews* with the Book of Mormon is not fair to either Ethan or Joseph Smith.[9] The following sample from Ethan's writings demonstrates this:

> One more argument I shall adduce from *facts* furnished in the Archaeology to show that the American natives are from the tribes of Israel. *The argument is a tradition of a trinity in the Great Spirit.* . . . An Indian article, called by this writer a "triune vessel," . . . an emblem of three of their principal gods, and seems to think of deriving an argument from it in favour of the natives being of East Indian extraction. He says of this triune vessel; "Does it not represent the three chief gods of India, Brahma, Vishnoo, and Siva." This certainly seems very far fetched! Why should they be supposed to be a representative of those three East Indian gods, any more than three other heathen gods on earth? Brahma, Vishnoo, and Siva are three distinct ideal gods. This *triune vessel* is one entire thing. It must rather then have been designed to represent one God with something like three faces, or characters.[10]

One would no more read Ethan Smith's book for doctrine than he would read the telephone directory in search of a plot. Trying to compare *View of the Hebrews* or Spaulding's *Manuscript Story* with the Book of Mormon is like trying to make something of the similarities in the musical notes used in both "Chopsticks" and Beethoven's Fifth Symphony!

However, the attacks on and efforts to undermine the Book of Mormon will doubtless continue. Those who cannot explain the book will try to diminish it in any way they can. Sad to say, a few seek to redefine the Book of Mormon in order to believe in it.

It is understandable that most of us still desire to know more about the Book of Mormon's coming forth, including its actual process of translation. This was certainly so with faithful and loyal Hyrum Smith. Upon Hyrum's suggesting that the

Prophet Joseph disclose such information to a group of assembled elders, Joseph told him "that it was not intended to tell the world all the particulars of the coming forth of the Book of Mormon . . . it was not expedient for him to relate these things."[11] Thus what we do know about the actual coming forth of the Book of Mormon is adequate, but it is not complete.

The real focus on the Book of Mormon should be on the details of the book itself, not on the details of the process by which it came forth. Although we do not know everything about the process of its coming forth or its translation, the Book of Mormon is open to full scrutiny.

Since the coming forth of the Book of Mormon amply fulfilled Isaiah's prophecy made centuries ago about a "marvellous work and a wonder" (Isaiah 29:14), let us consider some dimensions of how marvelous and wondrous it is.

Only the Prophet Joseph knew the full process of translation, and he was deliberately reluctant to supply details. So we take passing notice of the words of David Whitmer, Joseph Knight, and Martin Harris, who were observers, *not* translators. Whitmer indicated that by Joseph's using the divine instrumentalities "the hieroglyphics would appear, and also the translation in the English language . . . in bright luminous letters"; and Joseph would read the words off to Oliver, "who would write it down as spoken."[12] Martin Harris related of the seerstone, "sentences would appear and were read by the Prophet and written by Martin."[13] Joseph Knight reported similar descriptions of the process.[14]

Oliver Cowdery, who was much closer to the process, being involved daily as a scribe, is reported to have testified in court that the Urim and Thummim enabled Joseph "to read in English, the reformed Egyptian characters, which were engraved on the plates."[15]

If the above reports are accurate, they suggest a process indicative of God's having given Joseph "sight and power to translate" (D&C 3:12).[16]

If by means of these divine instrumentalities the Prophet was "seeing" ancient words rendered in English and then "dictating," Joseph was not simultaneously and constantly scrutinizing the characters on the actual plates—the usual translation process of going "back and forth" between pondering an ancient text and providing a modern rendering. The revelatory process was more crucial than the constant presence of opened plates, which, by instruction, were to be kept from the view of unauthorized eyes.

The revelatory process apparently did not require the Prophet to become expert in the ancient language.

While the use of divine instrumentalities might help to account for the rapid rate of translation, the procedure should not be regarded as merely mechanical (see D&C 9:8). In any case, we simply do not know the details; and, as indicated, Joseph was reluctant to describe details to his brother Hyrum or to anyone else.

The faith-filled process was not easy, however. This fact was clearly demonstrated in Oliver Cowdery's own attempt at translation. Oliver failed when he tried to translate, because he "did not continue as [he] commenced," and because, lacking faith and works, he "took no thought save it was to ask" (D&C 9:5–7). He "feared" (D&C 9:11) and just couldn't do it! Even so, we owe so much to Oliver Cowdery for his marvelous service as a scribe.

Whatever the details of the process, it required Joseph's intense, personal efforts along with the aid of the revelatory instruments. Moreover, the process itself may have varied as Joseph's capabilities grew, alternately involving the Urim and Thummim and the seerstone, with perhaps less reliance upon such instrumentalities in Joseph's later work of translation. Orson Pratt said Joseph Smith told him that he used the Urim and Thummim when he was inexperienced at translation, but later did not need it. This was certainly the case later in Joseph's inspired translation of verses in the Bible.[17]

Incrementally increased comprehension thus seems to be

a pattern by means of which the Lord stretches the capacity of His prophets.

The role of the divine instrumentalities provided should not be underestimated, however. For instance, anciently Abraham used the Urim and Thummim to view the galaxies. (See Abraham 3:1–4.)

Some additional things we know about the process of translation further qualify it as a "marvellous work and a wonder." One marvel, carefully set forth by John W. Welch, is the very rapidity with which Joseph was translating—at an estimated average rate of seven to ten of our printed pages per day![18] The total working time was about sixty-five to seventy-five working days.[19] By contrast, one able LDS translator in Japan, while surrounded by reference books and language dictionaries, and with translator colleagues available, has indicated that he considers an output of one careful, final page a day to be productive. And he is retranslating from earlier Japanese to modern Japanese! Over fifty able English scholars labored for seven years, using previous translations, to produce the King James Version of the Bible, averaging about one precious page per day. The Prophet would sometimes average ten pages per day![20]

From what we know, rarely would Joseph go back, review, or revise what he had already translated. The pages of the original Book of Mormon manuscript reflect a steady flow. The Prophet's "dictating" flowed, resulting—just as the compositor, John H. Gilbert, remembered—in an absence of paragraphing.

The process not only flowed, but it flowed at a very rapid rate under "the gift and power of God."

If a person were "manufacturing" or "borrowing" in such a situation, he would constantly need to cross-check, to edit, to revise for consistency. Had the Prophet dictated and then revised extensively, there would have been evidence of it. Thus, whatever its details, the translation process was astonishing.

Furthermore, Emma Smith said of the inspired process:

"When returning after meals, or after interruptions, [Joseph] would at once begin where he had left off, without either seeing the manuscript or having any portion of it read to him."[21] Usually, one who has dictated and been interrupted will resume by inquiring, "Now, where were we?" Not so with the Prophet!

Martin Harris—but no one else who participated or observed—is quoted as saying a blanket was hung between the scribe and Joseph. David Whitmer mentions a blanket being used, but only to partition off the living area in order to keep both translator and scribe from the eyes of visitors. However, Elizabeth Anne Whitmer Cowdery said, "Joseph never had a curtain drawn between him and his scribe."[22] Emma likewise said of her days as scribe, early on, that Joseph dictated "hour after hour with nothing between us."[23]

Of course, the real revelatory process involved Joseph's mind and required deep faith, things which could not be seen by others in any case.

Though translating an ancient record, Joseph himself was clearly unschooled in things ancient. For example, during the translation he came across words concerning a wall around Jerusalem and stopped and asked Emma whether there had been walls around Jerusalem. She affirmed that that was so.[24] Joseph simply hadn't known. Neither did he know of the literary form called chiasmus, which appears in the Bible at various places and, significantly, also in the Book of Mormon.

None of the people who either participated or merely observed (most of them the latter) mentions Joseph's having had any reference materials present.[25] Since the Prophet "dictated" openly, these individuals would have been aware of any unusual behavior or reliance upon other materials. Emma was emphatic on this very point: "He had neither manuscript nor book to read from. If he had had anything of the kind he could not have concealed it from me."[26] Emma does mention, and so does David Whitmer, the Prophet's spelling out loud unfamiliar names, for which there is evidence on the original manuscript itself.

Thus the Book of Mormon came *through* and not *from* Joseph Smith!

There is need for great care in suggesting that the Prophet had great flexibility as to doctrine and substance in the language he used. This may be gauged by Joseph's emphatic words about the title page of the Book of Mormon. "The title page of the Book of Mormon is a literal translation, taken from the very last leaf, on the left hand side of the collection or book of plates, which contained the record which has been translated; the language of the whole running the same as all Hebrew writing in general; and that, said title page is not by any means a modern composition either of mine or of any other man's who has lived or does live in this generation."[27]

Oliver Cowdery was the most constant and involved witness to the miraculous translation process, and he always affirmed the divinity of that process. Though disaffected from the Church for a time, he came humbly back by baptism into it. He spoke forthrightly as he said: "I wrote with my own pen the entire Book of Mormon (save a few pages) as it fell from the lips of the [p]rophet."[28] Oliver would not have humbly returned to the Church at all, especially seeking no station in it, had he been a party to any kind of fraud involving the Book of Mormon.

Even given his several years of disaffection, speaking of the Saints who by then had headquartered in a western valley, Oliver's testimony was that "[there] was no Salvation but in the valley and through the priesthood there."[29] At the time of his readmission, Oliver bore testimony of the Book of Mormon "in the same manner as is recorded in the testimony of the three witnesses," of whom he was one.[30]

At the approach of death, Oliver Cowdery couldn't have been more dramatic in his exit endorsement concerning the Book of Mormon. Of this experience, his half sister said: "Just before he breathed his last, he [Oliver] asked to be raised up in bed so he could talk to the family and friends and he told them to live according to the teachings in the [B]ook of Mormon and they would meet him in Heaven[. t]hen he said lay me down and let me fall asleep in the arms of Jesus, and he fell asleep without a struggle."[31]

The book's spiritual significance, of course, lies in its capacity for "convincing . . . Jew and Gentile that Jesus is the Christ." This is the very same reason as that given by the Apostle John for his testimony of the Savior's resurrection: "But these [signs] are written, that ye might believe that Jesus is the Christ, the Son of God; and that believing ye might have life through his name" (John 20:31).

This is why prophets write, whether John, Nephi, Mormon, or Moroni.

In 1829, especially while translating at an average rate that would produce seven to ten printed pages a day, Joseph would not have *fully* or *immediately* comprehended all the powerful and enhancing verses that were passing through him. One example of these is Alma 7:11–12, which represents a powerful addition to our understanding of Jesus' suffering and of His atonement and how it is that His empathy for each of us is perfect and very personal. Jesus understands the full range of human suffering. These and other insights were beyond Joseph Smith in 1829.

Likewise, in translating the substance of Alma 13:3 Joseph Smith was encountering, for the first time as far as we know, the doctrines of God's foreknowledge, man's premortal existence, and God's use of foreordination. Did Joseph fully and immediately understand all the implications of that verse which overturned the false doctrine of predestination? Bright as Joseph was, clearly he was encountering profound insights which he could not then have fully or immediately comprehended.

Since the plates had been so carefully assembled, edited, and preserved under God's direction, they were surely not destined to serve as a mere catalyst. Hence Joseph's mind was not permitted to trifle with divinely given doctrines! This observation is no discredit to Joseph Smith. On the contrary,

King Benjamin's words were not Benjamin's either, but "had been delivered unto him by the angel of the Lord" (Mosiah 4:1). Similarly, Nephi said of his words, "they are the words of Christ, and he hath given them unto me" (2 Nephi 33:10).

A further illustration of this particular point is that the Prophet Joseph Smith, while translating, especially if asked by the scribe, would spell—letter by letter—certain proper names. For instance, in his scribal duties Oliver Cowdery first wrote the name *Coriantumr* phonetically. He then crossed out his phonetic spelling and spelled the name as we now have it in the Book of Mormon. *Coriantumr*, with its unusual "mr" ending, clearly would have required a letter-by-letter spelling out loud by the Prophet.[32]

Why do we not have more disclosure concerning the process of translation? Perhaps because we would not be ready to understand it, even if it were given. Perhaps too because the Lord wants to leave the Book of Mormon in the realm of faith, though it is drenched with intrinsic evidence. Perhaps too because we are intended to immerse ourselves in the substance of the book itself rather than becoming unduly concerned with the process of its translation.

Furthermore, additional disclosures may actually depend upon how much we appreciate the previous divine disclosures. Writing under the Lord's direction, Mormon so indicated: "Then shall greater things be made manifest unto them. And if it so be that they will not believe these things, then shall the greater things be withheld from them, unto their condemnation. Behold, I was about to write them, all which were engraven upon the plates of Nephi, but the Lord forbade it, saying: *I will try the faith of my people.*" (3 Nephi 26:9–11, italics added; see also Mosiah 23:21.)

As soon as the translation process was completed, it was necessary for the Prophet Joseph to move on quickly in his very busy and highly compressed ministry. This ministry included fully establishing the Church, retranslating hundreds of verses in the Bible, and receiving various priesthood keys and heavenly messengers. Each of these brought new duties and new concerns: leading, for example to the winnowing Zion's Camp march and the calling and training of many Church leaders, including the Twelve and others as in the School of the Prophets.

It is notable that the Prophet Joseph sent nine of the Twelve to Britain on a proselyting mission when he could least afford to send them. Joseph also continued receiving various revelations; and he oversaw large gatherings of Church members in Kirtland, Ohio, Jackson County, Missouri, and Nauvoo, Illinois.

In addition, the Prophet experienced the awful and severe apostasy among members, especially in the Kirtland period and in Nauvoo. Wilford Woodruff reported that on one occasion he met Joseph in Kirtland and that for a while the Prophet said nothing but looked at him intently. Then the Prophet said, "Brother Woodruff, I am glad to see you. I hardly know when I meet those who have been my brethren in the Lord, who of them are my friends. They have become so scarce."[33]

All of this and much more combined to form Joseph's remarkable ministry. He finally focused on temple building and temple ordinances—in many ways the crowning achievement of his life.

Throughout all these experiences the Prophet Joseph was serving simultaneously as father and husband. He and Emma lost six of their natural or adopted children to early death. Finally, of course, came the engulfing events leading up to the martyrdom.

With so many large undertakings compressed into such a small period of time, the Prophet's ministry almost defies description. No wonder he once said that if he hadn't experienced his own life he would not have believed it.[34]

Yes, the precious Book of Mormon came *through* not *from* Joseph the Seer. Yes, it came to him by the "gift and power of God." But, no, it was not "his" book, even though he was its remarkable translator! It was actually the book of prophets who had long before preceded him. By means of his intensive labors of translation Joseph has let these prophets speak eloquently for themselves—to millions of us. More printed pages of scripture have come through Joseph Smith than through any other human!

Near the end of his ministry, with so much betrayal about him, the Prophet Joseph said to the members, "I never told you I was perfect; but there is no error in the revelations which I have taught."[35] This summational statement includes the marvelous Book of Mormon, the coming forth of which we have here examined briefly.

Jesus, the great Redeemer of mankind, called the Prophet Joseph Smith and tutored and nurtured him through his adversities, which were for but "a small moment" (D&C 121:7).

The Prophet Joseph once hoped aloud that he might so live, amid his suffering, that one day he could take his place among Abraham and the "ancients," hoping to "hold an even weight in the balances with them."[36] Joseph indeed so triumphed, which is why we can rightly sing of his being "crowned in the midst of the prophets of old."[37]

We can have faith in the Restoration scriptures, which in turn do so much to increase our faith in all facets of the gospel, including its sacred ordinances.

CHAPTER

5

Faith in
Gospel Ordinances

The revealed ordinances of the gospel of Jesus Christ
were designed, from the beginning, to develop and to certify
individuals who are prepared to "go home" to our Father to
receive the "fulness of the Father," even "all that [He] hath"
(D&C 76:71; see also 84:38). We can and should have faith
in these saving ordinances, just as we do in Him whose prescribed ordinances they are. The ordinances are not merely
quaint and reminding rituals. They are essential, both for the
"here and now" and to qualify us for the "there and then."

Since God is no respecter of persons, these ordinances are
democratically available to all the worthy—without reference
to whether one is rich or poor, brown, black, or white, and re-
gardless of vocation, education, social status, or any other
earthly measures of standing. The emerging Saints who have
been blessed by these ordinances and who have kept their
covenants in connection therewith will be those who, in King
Benjamin's words, are "submissive, meek, humble, patient,
[and] full of love" (Mosiah 3:19). The ordinances of the gospel,
especially temple ordinances, help to produce this special, spiritual cadre.

Of Jesus during His mortal messiahship it was said that "the common people heard him gladly" (Mark 12:37). The saving ordinances of the temple are for all worthies, including "the common people" and those whom the world regards as "weak" and "foolish" (1 Corinthians 1:27). James wrote that God has "chosen the poor of this world, rich in faith" (James 2:5). Gospel ordinances truly are for those "rich in faith," even though these sacred and vital ordinances remain unappreciated by the world and are even mocked by some.

Why do we need outward ordinances, anyway? God surely knows our inner thoughts and feelings, our hearts, minds, and intentions, and can judge us perfectly. So why not judge us without reference to any outward ordinances? After all, some in the world regard themselves as Christians but disdain any ordinances at all.

Ordinances, in fact, are required for several vital reasons. To begin with, ordinances show our visible, outward obedience to the Lord and His plan of salvation.

Though sinless, Jesus Himself was baptized "to fulfil all righteousness" (Matthew 3:15). Nephi further declared that Jesus, whose humility was total and whose submissiveness was complete, thus "showeth unto the children of men that, . . . he humbleth himself before the Father, and witnesseth unto the Father that he would be obedient unto him in keeping his commandments. . . . [Showing] unto the children of men the straitness of the path, and the narrowness of the gate, by which they should enter, he having set the example before them." (2 Nephi 31:7, 9.) Nothing could be more plain!

We note this corresponding teaching by Joseph Smith: "If a man gets the fulness of God he has to get [it] in the same way that Jesus Christ obtained it and that was by keeping all the ordinances of the house of the Lord."[1]

There really are no exceptions!

Even after Paul had his spectacular spiritual experience on the road to Damascus, the first instruction he received was to go to Ananias in order to be taught and prepared for baptism and for his later labors (see Acts 9).

President Brigham Young confirmed that outward ordinances demonstrate our obedience to God. "How shall we know that we obey Him? There is but one method by which we can know it, and that is by the inspiration of the Spirit of the Lord witnessing unto our spirit that we are His, that we love Him, and that He loves us. It is by the spirit of revelation we know this. We have no witness to ourselves internally, without the spirit of revelation. We have no witness outwardly only by obedience to the ordinances."[2]

Hence ordinances are required not because God lacks the omniscience needed to know our true spiritual status, but because we need to make visible, outward compliance for our own sakes. One day, when the Book of Life is opened, it will be incontestably shown, along with our other defining deeds, that we actually participated in certain ordinances, and also what our subsequent pattern of living was in connection with each ordinance and its associated covenants.

On Judgment Day, not only will every knee bow and every tongue confess that Jesus is the Christ but also, as elaborating Book of Mormon prophets tell us, everyone, including those who have lived without God in the world, will also openly acknowledge that God is God and will confess before God that His judgments are just and merciful (see Mosiah 16:1; 27:31; Alma 12:15). Part of the basis for demonstrating the perfection of God's justice and mercy will thus be the cumulative record which we ourselves will have made (see Alma 41:7). Out of this we can be justly judged, a judgment that will include our compliance with outward gospel ordinances with all their respective covenants.

Furthermore, when we worthily participate in ordinances there actually are specific effects, sometimes immediate ones. A baptism worthily received, for instance, really does thereby cleanse the participant of past sins. What an immense relief! A sealing worthily entered into actually does unite a man and a woman for time and for all eternity. What a companionship! These effects are saving and salutary, and, as President Brigham Young declared, we can thus "know for ourselves the saving effects they produce in mankind."[3] Coming to know for ourselves—really know—is so much a part of the plan of salvation.

Additionally, ordinances are intended to cast our minds forward to specific promises and to our developmental possibilities. In Brigham Young's words: "When we obey the commandments of our heavenly Father, if we have a correct understanding of the ordinances of the house of God, we receive all the promises attached to the obedience rendered to His commandments."[4]

Temple and other ordinances help us greatly to see "things as they really are" and "as they really will be" (Jacob 4:13).

Ordinances mark the path of our rigorous, personal journey. The periodic repetition of certain ordinances is needed to remind us of who we are and where we should be going.

Furthermore, meekly submitting to ordinances also constitutes an open submittal to authority as held by those God has called to administer His ordinances. This is no small thing in an age of general revolution against any authority at all and of so much rebellion against traditional standards. Thereby, like our Savior, we also show the children of men that we humble ourselves before the Father's servants who administer the ordinances in His behalf (see 2 Nephi 31:7, 9).

Ordinances likewise serve to acknowledge submittal to God's timetable, since "all things must come to pass in their time" (D&C 64:32). In some ways, each ordinance is a marker, suggesting where we are or should be, at least approximately, on the pathway of our personal development. Let us be careful, therefore, not to look "beyond the mark" (Jacob 4:14).

Ordinances thus blend faith and works. They are not, however, rituals which save all by themselves, that is, if unaided by the righteous life. Covenants must be kept before blessings flow. On the other hand, random goodness, unaccompanied by divine ordinances, is not of full salvational effect either: "Wherefore he that prayeth, whose spirit is contrite, the same is accepted of me if he obey mine ordinances" (D&C 52:15).

Ordinances are so personal. Of this Joseph Smith further declared: "Reading the experience of others, or the revelation given to *them*, can never give *us* a comprehensive view of our condition and true relation to God. Knowledge of these things can only be obtained by experience through the ordinances of God set forth for that purpose."[5] We can thus increase our personal faith "by experience," "through the ordinances of God."

Ordinances that are faithfully submitted to and complied with, unsurprisingly, also have a sifting effect among individuals. Speaking of when the fulness of the gospel is preached, Erastus Snow taught:

> It always did produce a separation between the righteous and the wicked. It drew the line of distinction. . . . It sets Saints to running together. It works out apostates from among us, and they take the opposite direction. It draws the line of distinction between the righteous and the wicked, . . . But while the wicked on the one hand are thus filling up their cup of iniquity, the righteous, on the other hand are called to sanctify themselves and be prepared for the glorious coming of the Savior. It is for this cause that we build temples, and that God reveals to us the ordinances for the sanctification of His people and further glory and exaltation.[6]

More than we realize, ordinances comprise defining moments of record!

The comparative few in this world who are privileged and worthy to go to the holy temple are, in fact, "the salt of the earth." Hence the great concern we should have in the Church about the salt losing its savor.

President Brigham Young said of our perilous time, "It was revealed to me in the commencement of this Church, that the Church would spread, prosper, grow and extend, and that in proportion to the spread of the Gospel among the nations of the earth, so would the power of Satan rise."[7] The pervasive and vexing challenge of growing wickedness makes reminding and reassuring gospel ordinances even more of an individual imperative.

According to the Prophet Joseph Smith, the crucial holy endowment was administered to Moses "on the mountaintop."[8] President Joseph Fielding Smith expressed the belief that Peter, James, and John also received the holy endowment on a mountain, the Mount of Transfiguration.[9] Nephi, too, was caught up to an exceedingly high mountain (see 1 Nephi 11:1) and was instructed not to write or speak of some of the things he experienced there (see 1 Nephi 14:25). Did something similar occur to him at that time?

Since we are to strive to prepare in this life for return to and reunion with our Father in Heaven, ordinances open that door. C. S. Lewis wrote perceptively: "Our life-long nostalgia, our longing to be reunited with something in the universe from which we now feel cut off, to be on the inside of some door which we have always seen from the outside, is . . . the truest index of our real situation."[10]

Jacob speaks of this moment of admission and reconciliation: "O . . . come unto the Lord, the Holy One. Remember that . . . the keeper of the gate is the Holy One of Israel; and he employeth no servant there. . . . And whoso knocketh, to him will he open." (2 Nephi 9:41–42.)

Particularly appropriate is the Lord's declaration, "I will hasten my work in its time" (D&C 88:73). When God hastens His work, He hastens it on both sides of the veil simultaneously. No wonder holy temples, such a central feature of the Restoration, are so crucial, especially at this juncture in human history. Whenever, as is now happening, we open to gospel proselyting new nations on this side of the veil, we have simultaneously opened the door to thousands of one-time citizens of those nations who are now living beyond the veil of death. Vicarious ordinances provide that precious spiritual linkage of love.

How large is the Lord's work? There are now nearly nine million members of the Church living on the earth. However, there are also several million members of the Church beyond the veil. It is likewise expansive to learn that God's work is not confined to this one planet. We do not worship a one-planet God! The Lord told Moses, however, "but only an account of this earth, and the inhabitants thereof, give I unto you" (Moses 1:35). Even so, the Lord has told us some soaring things: "By [Christ], . . . the worlds are and were created, and the inhabitants thereof are begotten sons and daughters unto God" (D&C 76:24).

The Lord has created "worlds without number" for His announced purpose (Moses 1:33, 39). The theology of the Restoration is not tied to any particular theories of astrophysics but is expansive and takes account of an expansive universe as it gives us a few inklings.

For instance, astronomers say they have discovered an "enormous wall . . . of galaxies . . . the largest structure yet observed in the universe."[11]

These scientists say of the recent discoveries, "We keep seeing something bigger as we go out farther."[12] Latter-day Saints should not be surprised, however, because the Lord has said there is "no end to my works" (Moses 1:38).

There is pattern and order in the universe. Kolob "standeth above the earth," Abraham was told, "and govern[s] all those which belong to the same order as that upon which thou standest" (Abraham 3:1–5). Scientists say the newly discovered nonrandom "galaxies appear to be arranged in a network of strings, or filaments, surrounding large, relatively empty regions of space known as voids."[13]

Furthermore, "our galaxy, the Milky Way, is located in one of the relatively empty spaces between the great walls."[14] Significantly, the Lord told Abraham of this earth's being located: "there is space there, and we will . . . make an earth" (Abraham 3:24).

One eminent scientist is quoted as saying, "As we look out into the Universe and identify the many accidents of physics and astronomy that have worked together to our benefit, it almost seems as if the Universe must in some sense have known that we were coming."[15]

The Lord's work is very, very large! Truly, "The heavens declare the glory of God; and the firmament sheweth his handywork" (Psalm 19:1). Despite this vastness, Enoch affirmed to God, "Yet thou art there" (Moses 7:30).

What we learn in temples tells us about the plurality of worlds as well as our true identities and our genuine possibilities; all of which is reminiscent of the lyrics of a lovely song (over which the lyricist reportedly worked through many drafts):

> On a clear day, rise and look around you,
> And you'll see who you are.
> On a clear day, how it will astound you—
> That the glow of your being outshines every star . . .
> And on a clear day . . .
> You can see forever and ever more.*

It is always a "clear day" in the holy temples of God. Gospel ordinances help us to "see who we are." We can "see forever." We can see who others are.

Painfully conscious as we are of our many inadequacies, it is especially emancipating and ennobling to be regarded not

---

* From "On a Clear Day You Can See Forever." Words by Alan Jay Lerner, music by Burton Lane. Copyright © 1965 by Alan Jay Lerner and Burton Lane. Chappell & Co. owner of publication and allied rights throughout the world. International copyright secured. All rights reserved.

alone for what we now are but also for what we have the power to become. Gospel ordinances help show the way more than we now know.

Amid such cosmic vastness, can we exhibit sufficient daily discipleship that our faith will fail not?

CHAPTER

6

Faith That
Fails Not

From both the principle and the process of faith there are no exemptions, even for prophets. Failure of faith is a persistent possibility for all.

When counseling Peter, Jesus said he had prayed for Peter "that thy faith fail not." Jesus further noted that Peter still needed to be fully "converted." (Luke 22:32.) President Brigham Young observed that the Prophet Joseph Smith "had to pray all the time, exercise faith, live his religion, and magnify his calling, to obtain the manifestations of the Lord, and to keep him steadfast in the faith."[1]

No wonder the Lord selects as His presiding prophets men of proven faith. Orson Hyde gave us a special reassurance, saying:

> When an individual is ordained and appointed to lead the people, he has passed through tribulations and trials, and has proven himself before God, and before his people, that he is worthy of the situation which he holds. . . . A person that has not been tried, that has not proved himself before God, and before his people, and before the councils of the Most High . . .

is not going to step in to lead the Church and people of God. . . . Someone that understands the Spirit and counsel of the Almighty, that knows the Church, and is known of her, is the character that will lead the Church.[2]

One major reason for the various reminders to us about avoiding the failure of our faith is the war within the soul, the war between the flesh and the individual spirit (see 1 Peter 2:11). Paul laid it out candidly and specifically: "For the flesh lusteth against the Spirit, and the Spirit against the flesh: and these are contrary the one to the other: so that ye cannot do the things that ye would" (Galatians 5:17).

When Jesus observed his sleeping Apostles in the Garden of Gethsemane, He commented that "the spirit indeed is willing, but the flesh is weak" (Matthew 26:41). His comment was more than a kindly commentary on sleeping Apostles who would have desired to stay awake; it was a tremendous insight which clearly pertains to life and to faith.

When we read in the scriptures of man's "weakness," this term includes the generic but necessary weakness inherent in the general human condition in which the flesh has such an incessant impact upon the spirit (see Ether 12:28–29). Weakness likewise includes, however, our specific, individual weaknesses, which we are expected to overcome (see D&C 66:3; Jacob 4:7). Life has a way of exposing these weaknesses. If we are meek, what is an individual weakness can later even become a strength. Hence the Lord said, "I give unto men weakness that they may be humble" (Ether 12:27). For those who seek to live by celestial principles, however, the basic conflict between the flesh and the spirit will go on, individually, until the flesh is finally subdued (see Galatians 5:16–25).

The eventual and eternal reunion of body and spirit, when these are inseparably connected after the resurrection, will bring a glorious fulness of joy (see D&C 93:33). Until then, however, we are, said Brigham, "encumbered with this flesh," with its "weakness, blindness, and lethargy." The constraints of the flesh contribute to our "disposition to weep or mourn."[3] So much of our "fear and trembling" arises from anxieties which drive us "to know how to save ourselves pertaining to the flesh."[4] Even our fear of trials continued, said President Young, "is on account of [our] tabernacles," so "while we are in the flesh the Gospel is calculated to deliver those who live by its principles from all those fears,"[5] whereas the Spirit has "no disposition to weep or mourn."

Hence Jesus' utterance, "the spirit indeed is willing, but the flesh is weak," is a profound declaration and not merely an observation about sleepy Apostles. If we but reflect on the process, we realize that our bodily fears and anxieties often do focus on pain, hunger, deprivation, fatigue, and even death. These are certainly natural to the natural man. The natural man, by the way, is very much at home in a consumer society, for "in a consumer society there are inevitably two kinds of slaves: the prisoners of addiction, and the prisoners of envy."[6]

Noting the challenges of the flesh does not require that we denigrate the remarkable physical body, the acquisition and care of which are part of the plan of salvation.

Homeostasis, the state of being in equilibrium, is most commonly used when speaking of the body. For example, the normal human body temperature is around 98.6 degrees Fahrenheit. If a person exerts himself, the heart rate increases and the body perspires in order to maintain the desired temperature level. Similarly, if the person is in a very cold environment, such as when skiing, the body shivers to maintain the appropriate temperature. Other mechanisms keep breathing, heart rate, and other body functions within narrowly defined limits. However, the homeostatic mechanisms can be overcome by disease. Bacterial infections, for example, will increase the body temperature above the normal range, in which case some remedial action is needed.

The spirit, too, should be in a state of homeostasis. It too has mechanisms that, if heeded, will keep it within the Lord's prescribed bounds. Daily prayer, regular reading of the scriptures, attendance at Church meetings, and serving one's fellowman are ways of nurturing the soul by keeping it in "spiritual homeostasis." Another "mechanism" is fasting—an effective reminder to us of the need to have the spirit dominate the body as the latter asserts its need for food and water. If the spirit is overcome by the disease of transgression, it will become ill, reflecting guilt, remorse, or a feeling of spiritual malaise. Remedial action such as repentance can restore the soul to its homeostatic state.

Calling attention to those appetites of the flesh which can sicken us is thus not intended to suggest that our bodies are unimportant, nor to depreciate the need to take care of those remarkable and necessary bodies wisely. It is instead to emphasize that yielding to certain appetites of the flesh, if these are untamed or unchecked by the spirit, will lead to grave difficulty and misery that include harm to the physical body. Little wonder that the adversary ever strives to influence us through the weaknesses of the flesh.

Jesus counseled, "Fear not them which kill the body, but are not able to kill the soul: but rather fear him which is able to destroy both soul and body in hell" (Matthew 10:28). Once such enemies have done whatever they will to the body, they "have no more that they can do" (Luke 12:4). Paul understood this, urging "that we may boldly say, The Lord is my helper, and I will not fear what man shall do unto me" (Hebrews 13:6).

Peter's temporary denial of his friendship with Jesus occurred because of the fear of men, who had actually done nothing to him at that time but clearly might have (see Mark 14:66–72). Mere "fear of persecution" causes some to falter (see D&C 40:2). Brigham Young so observed: "People suffer more in the anticipation of death, than in death itself. There is more suffering in what I call borrowed trouble, than in the trouble itself."[7]

"I" is sometimes called the "vertical pronoun." The nearly constant and almost reflexive emphasis on *I* should help us see how persistent and pervasive the flesh is. We say, "I am thirsty," "I am tired," and "I am hungry," indicating that the very assertiveness of the flesh itself makes us self-centered. Therefore, we usually think in terms of meeting "my needs"; it is "my turn"; it is "my property"; and "it is my body." The various stimuli which steadily flow from the flesh ensure that we will spend much of our time thinking about ourselves, often well beyond what is genuinely needed. The solution is to yield more and more to the spirit rather than to the flesh.

So it is that *I*, while a straight and narrow letter itself, has great difficulty walking the straight and narrow path! This calling attention to the power of the flesh is intended neither to intimidate nor to excuse us. But we do need to recognize there is an ongoing war between the flesh and the spirit, and hence we will do well to know the enemy's "order of battle." Each lessening of the influence of the flesh upon our faith brings increasing success in our becoming valiant.

The persistent assertions of the flesh virtually ensure that as soon as our immediate needs and appetites have been satisfied we will forget the satisfaction. Thus ancient Israel had its thirst quenched by miraculous means, only to murmur again later on when they were thirsty once more. Hence clear and sharp spiritual memories are needed to operate as an effective antidote by blunting the insistence of the flesh.

Sexual immorality, for instance, represents a bow before the selfish needs of the flesh, bringing "remorse, the fatal egg by pleasure laid."[8] How many times hearts have thus painfully died, "pierced with deep wounds," to use the powerful language of Jacob? (See Jacob 2:35.) Lust uses another person and then leaves such tragic human debris, as, in Cowper's words, "Men deal with life as children with their play,/Who first misuse, then cast their toys away."[9]

We cannot safely trust "in the arm of flesh." Even when it is pumped full of steroids, it lacks the strength to maintain its grasp on the iron rod. Not alone does the arm of flesh finally prove anemic, but it always reaches for the wrong things (see 2 Chronicles 32:8; Jeremiah 17:5).

President Young observed that "the fear and trembling, the misgivings and wavering arise from the anxiety [about] how to save ourselves pertaining to the flesh. That weakness is not exhibited in the spirit."[10] Thus, "the flesh," if it overcomes, brings the spirit into sad bondage. But, said President Young, "if the spirit overcomes, the body is made free, and then we are free indeed."[11]

Again, the point is not to excuse ourselves because of the flesh but to allow for the power of the flesh by avoiding those situations which could exploit the natural weaknesses of the flesh.

Most important, however, we should strengthen and nourish the inner man by keeping on the straight and narrow path.

Lust and fatigue are such common weaknesses of the flesh. Even the impact of moods upon our faith probably reflects the influence of the flesh as well. The adversary knows our pattern of moods. He can and does exploit them, as in the matter of our inability to control our impulses, or our added vulnerability when discouraged. In these ways, "the will of the flesh [gives] . . . the spirit of the devil power to captivate . . . that he may reign over you" (2 Nephi 2:29).

No wonder Peter said, "For of whom a man is overcome, of the same is he brought into bondage" (2 Peter 2:19). We are conquered by whatever incorrectly and sufficiently obsesses us, including by all the subtle forms of bondage (see 1 Peter 2:20). But always the Lord holds out to us the way to freedom (see D&C 98:8; John 8:36; 1 Corinthians 10:13).

One could be brought into "bondage" not only by lust but also by undue concern over status, or by hunger for recognition. Likewise, one could be brought into bondage by the craving to dominate or to possess material things, or by the allure of sensualism's many faces.

The "natural man" is not free. For instance, in his limiting myopia it is not natural for him to be sensitive to the needs of those who are *behind* or *below* him. By way of simple example, our striving to get ahead in vehicular traffic is usually done without worrying about the person behind us.

Organizational charts often encourage us to be humble "up" but less humble toward those who are "down." The natural man simply faces in the wrong direction, and in every way his appetites of the flesh take him farther and farther away from God. "For how knoweth a man the master whom he has not served, and who is a stranger unto him, and is far from the thoughts and intents of his heart?" (Mosiah 5:13.) We must serve Jesus in order to come to know him.

The natural man fears being "taken in" by trusting another. The flesh is unduly concerned too with outward appearances and with the opinions of the world. Would that we all would be equally concerned with, even "shake at," the appearance of sin! (See 2 Nephi 4:31.)

When we are yielding to God—submitting to His plan of salvation, applying Jesus' atonement to ourselves, and emulating His character, appreciating the Restoration—these, the conditions of our "original assent," do not need to be constantly reexamined. Some of little faith suppose otherwise, of course. In fact, once one has submitted to the process of faith, understanding is enlightened, and the mind is expanded (see Alma 32:34). Faith provides its own genuine evidence and its own renewal. Faith even moves us further on to a state of knowledge in some things.

By not being actively involved in the process of faith, doubters simply do not receive reinforcing rewards. They also resent the lack of sympathetic vibrations from the faithful each time doubters themselves oscillate in response to what they suppose is some "new evidence" to the contrary. C. S. Lewis made the point that those without faith are entitled to dispute with those who have faith about the grounds of their "original assent," but doubters should not be surprised if "after the assent has been given, our adherence to it is no longer proportioned to every fluctuation of the apparent evidence."[12]

Day by day the faithful garner more of the substance of things hoped for and accumulate more evidence or assurance of things not seen (see JST Hebrews 11:1). Doubters may not really desire to believe—or at least believe sufficiently to give place in their lives to plant the word. Doubtless they do not allow, either, for God's comprehending so many things that mortals do not comprehend (see Hebrews 11:6; Mosiah 4:9). Paul's litany of the faithful describes how "these all . . . were persuaded . . . and embraced" God's promises with full faith (Hebrews 11:13). Forlorn doubters want the full harvest of faith but without the full work of farming faith.

The Spirit can teach us of "things as they really are"—not just as they appear to be, according to conventional wisdom. Contrariwise, the flesh looks at the outward things, drawing its conclusions from surface appearances (see 1 Samuel 16:7). The *opinions* of the flesh, it turns out, are no more reliable than the *arm* of flesh! Faith, meanwhile, carries us forward even before the full flood of fact reaches and lifts us. Since meekness is not natural to the natural man, however, we must "learn" some things over and over again—until we get it right! Faith and meekness make allowance for the role of such repeated experiences in Father's plan. Repetition is part of God's long-suffering in our behalf.

Whether or not we acknowledge it, our constant dependence should be on God, who gives us breath from moment to moment (see Mosiah 2:21). Why do we not see the clear connection between our being given "breath . . . from one moment to another" and God's promise to the faithful that their years and days shall not be numbered less? (See D&C 122:9.) God who oversees the first process also oversees the corresponding timetable. He "is in the details" of individual lives as well as in the details of galaxies and molecules.

Our fleshly failure to so see "things as they really are, and . . . as they really will be" is one root problem inherent in a condition of "little faith." For example, we may mistakenly think, as some did anciently in Israel, "Mine [own] hand hath gotten me this wealth" (Deuteronomy 8:17). It is our provinciality—the framework of the flesh instead of the framework of faith—which leads us to be confused about causality.

We falter too when our highest priority is not assigned to the first commandment. We forget to whom our first duties lie. Eli was a commendable and serviceable prophet; nevertheless, he could not restrain his "vile" sons (see 1 Samuel 3:13). Eli may have grown understandably weary of trying, given what was probably daily disappointment with the behavior of his sons. Yet, good man that he was, Eli still recognized the voice of God when it called Samuel (see 1 Samuel 3:8).

When sharp differences arose, Elder Thomas B. Marsh couldn't restrain his wife's ego (or his own) regarding the fair sharing of milk among neighbors as previously agreed; hence he lost his apostleship and, for many years, his Church membership. Big mistakes are made over such little things! Little sparks can start such big bonfires. It is well that the sturdy shield of faith can be used not only to quench fiery darts (see Ephesians 6:16) but also to extinguish the small sparks struck by the flint of frustration. In daily life the shield of faith must be ever ready as well as ever sturdy.

Often faith falters because we have become offended. When the moment of offense comes, we feel put down, unappreciated, unvalued, not understood, or dealt with unjustly. And we may actually have been dealt with unfairly or insensitively! But if we have faith in our true identity and in our loving God's purposes for us we can better deal with genuine disappointments even when our faith and patience are tried simultaneously (see Mosiah 23:21).

Brigham Young sustained the Prophet Joseph supernally. Only once, he said, did he question the Prophet—and that briefly and not over a spiritual matter. "I never called him in question, even in my feelings, for an act of his, except once. I did not like his policy in a matter, and a feeling came into my heart that would have led to complain; but it was much shorter lived than Jonah's gourd, for it did not last half a minute. Much of Joseph's policy in temporal things was different from my ideas of the way to manage them."[13]

Thus failures of faith may reflect failures to submit to the "Lord's anointed," perhaps out of resentment that they not "rule over us" (2 Nephi 5:3; see also Numbers 16:13). Apostasy is more than doubt; it is sometimes actual "mutiny," just as the Apostle John experienced it from Diotrephes (see 3 John 1:9–10). The defections and betrayals in the Kirtland and the Nauvoo periods represented mutiny. So many people "piled on" by being disloyal to the Prophet. Not everyone was a Hyrum or a Brigham or a Wilford.

A few in the Church today choose to meet their defining moments by separating themselves from the Church and its leaders. A few set themselves up in open rebellion as a substitute light (see 2 Nephi 26:29).

The Lord will tend and tutor His anointed. He has His special ways, and we can trust Him to manage His leaders. Meanwhile those same leaders, whether Moses or Brigham Young, humbly and genuinely wish that every man were a prophet and each individual could have his own strong witness that this work is true (see Numbers 11:29; D&C 1:20).

Some have difficulty, however, about reposing confidence in the Lord's anointed. Over the decades, "we have learned by sad experience" that it is better for developing dissidents to be lovingly counseled, and, if necessary, lovingly disciplined "early on." Often, waiting means that any meekness they have vanishes. It is sad that, as their faith shrinks, their circle of influence may temporarily enlarge. From Liberty Jail, the Prophet Joseph, who had known so much betrayal and learned from so much "sad experience," declared his determination thus: "Your humble servant or servants, intend from henceforth to disapprobate everything that is not in accordance with the fullness of the Gospel of Jesus Christ, . . . They will not hold their peace— as in times past when they see iniquity beginning to rear its head—for fear of traitors, or the consequences that shall follow by reproving those who creep in unawares, that they may get something with which to destroy the flock."[14]

A few in the Church simply don't like to have anybody preside over them. They are like the critics of Nephi, who complained that "Nephi thinks to rule over us," saying that power, instead, "belongs unto us" (2 Nephi 5:3). It was the same in Moses' time. Dissidents "rose up" against Moses, complaining, "thou . . . make thyself . . . a prince over us. . . . Ye take too much upon you." (Numbers 16:2, 3, 13.) Some complained then—and a few do now—"Hath the Lord indeed spoken only by Moses? hath he not spoken also by us?" (Numbers 12:2.)

In fact, Moses "was very meek, above all the men which were upon the face of the earth" (Numbers 12:3). He understood the principles set forth centuries later in section 121 of the Doctrine and Covenants. Moses had enough faith in Jesus to forego the riches of Egypt (see Hebrews 11:26). He also had enough faith in the rich principles of Jesus' gospel to let those principles improve him and mold him.

Our individual years and days, too, will not be numbered less in God's plan and timetable, if we are faithful (see D&C 122:9). Whether experiencing a severe wind on Galilee (see Matthew 8:23–27), or a fierce wind on the high seas such as pounded Lehi's vessel (see 1 Nephi 18:15), or the turbulence in our own lives, it is the same. If we know Jesus is our Lord and that He watches over us, we can handle—though we will surely feel them—all the winds of strange doctrines and all the surging commotion (see Matthew 24:23–28).

Failures of faith mirror basic deficiencies, as in ancient Israel: "And he said, . . . for they are a very froward generation, children in whom is no faith" (Deuteronomy 32:20). The word *froward* denotes perversity, but it also denotes "self-willed" and "devoid of loyalty."

The present is a time of significant numerical and spiritual growth in the Church. We shouldn't be surprised, however, if it is also a time of some sifting. Sifting is usually self-initiated, and it is going on all the time. There are ways leading into the Church, and there are ways leading out. The influence and tug of the world is always present; but especially since the world grows more boldly wicked, this sharper defining has a greater and more visible effect on some of little faith.

Fortunately, so many Church members are full of faith and are spiritually mature. A few, being unsettled, seem to prefer living within the zones of excitation or titillation, hence they can be easily misled or diverted into hobbies, and their faith can fail. Surely one thing in which we need not develop more faith is our or someone else's religious hobby.

How quickly and easily the few are misled! Such members may know superficially of the doctrines of the kingdom, but their root system is shallow. Though able to provide doctrinal recitation, they seem not to know either the implications or interconnections of those doctrines.

For instance, instead of wisely noticing the warning leaves on the fig tree, a few proceed to fixate on the specific timing of Jesus' second coming. Yet the Savior clearly stated, "But of that day and hour knoweth no man, no, not the angels of heaven, but my Father only" (Matthew 24:36).

Clearly, since even the angels in heaven—an otherwise reasonably well-informed group—do not know, we should be wary of mortals obsessed with calendaring. So often modern gnostics who in one exotic way or another pretend to be "in the know" are, in fact, spiritually "out of touch"! Meanwhile, mature members will take time both to smell the flowers and also watch the leaves on the fig tree to see when "summer is nigh" (Matthew 24:32–33).

Granted, some events preceding the second coming of Jesus are already under way, but we mustn't be so caught up with associated concerns that we lose our balance. The premature expectation of the Second Coming has been a frequent error. Discernment is especially needed in a time when the wheat and tares exist side by side. One can recognize the genuine disciples, since the faith of these individuals is increasing. They are visibly improving and becoming more like Jesus. These can be known by their fruits, not by their hobbies. Because these faithful disciples are winning the war of the spirit over the flesh, we see in them the fruits of victory: love, joy, peace, long-suffering, gentleness, goodness, faith, meekness, and temperance (see Galatians 5:22–23).

The "works of the flesh" are equally apparent, however, bringing sexual immorality, dissension, sedition, heresies, sadness, and misery (see Galatians 5:19–21). After all, "wickedness never was happiness" (Alma 41:10) and never will be.

Other special guidance is available to help ensure that our faith does not fail. We sustain (several times a year) fifteen men as prophets, seers, and revelators. They are, in our time, those to whom to look for guidance. There are a few members of the Church, however, who withhold support in one way or another, and who "set themselves up for a light" and "seek not the welfare of Zion" (2 Nephi 26:29).

Yet we need not be prey to pretenders or detractors, especially in view of the fact that "the day cometh that they who will not hear the voice of the Lord, neither the voice of his servants, neither give heed to the words of the prophets and apostles, shall be cut off from among the people" (D&C 1:14).

The faithful will not be restless. The lame man was instructed by the two Apostles, "Look on us. And he gave heed unto them." (Acts 3:4–5.) So it should be with Church members today. President George Q. Cannon, as if speaking of the few members in the zone of excitation, observed: "Apostates have asserted that there was not the power in the leaders of the Church which there should be. . . . There are some members of the Church who have appeared to think that there has been some power lacking, and have manifested a feeling of restlessness, anticipating the rising of some one who should have greater authority than at present exists. . . . The apostleship, now held in this Church, embodies all the authority bestowed by the Lord upon man in the flesh."[15]

The very process of Church government also assures us

that we do not have secret leaders. "It shall not be given to any one to go forth to preach my gospel, or to build up my church, except he be ordained by some one who has authority, and it is known to the church that he has authority and has been regularly ordained by the heads of the church" (D&C 42:11).

Elder Wilford Woodruff counseled the Church flock: "The very moment that men in this kingdom attempt to run ahead or cross the path of their leaders, no matter in what respect, the moment they do this they are in danger of being injured by the wolves. . . . I have never in my life known it to fail, that when men went contrary to the counsel of their leaders, either in the days of Joseph or Brother Brigham, they always became entangled and suffered a loss by so doing."[16]

We have been given apostles and prophets not only "for the perfecting of the Saints" but also to make sure that we are "no more children, tossed to and fro, and carried about with every wind of doctrine" (Ephesians 4:11–14). Apostolic watchcare over the doctrines of the kingdom, in order to keep them pure, is a very important duty. The performance of that important duty should be expected, not resented.

The lack of faith and confidence in the Lord's leaders almost inevitably brings a loss of personal faith. Of this challenge, Elder George A. Smith observed: "Some men in their hours of darkness may feel—I have heard of men feeling so—that the work is about done, that the enemies of the Saints have become so powerful, and bring such vast wealth and energy to bear against them that we are all going to be crushed out pretty soon. I will say to such brethren, it is very bad policy for you, because you think the old ship Zion is going to sink, to jump overboard."[17]

As critics become more clever and enemies more numerous, let us remember and be reassured by the resurrected Jesus' promise: "My wisdom is greater than the cunning of the devil" (3 Nephi 21:10). Talk of desirable perspective! One major deprivation of the adversary is that he simply does not know the "mind of Christ" (1 Corinthians 2:16; see also Moses 4:6).

No wonder Paul advises us that what is needed is "repentance to the acknowledging of the truth" (2 Timothy 2:25). Facing up to gospel truths is not easy for the natural man, since he prefers playing in his local sandpile rather than contemplating the cosmos and thereby seeing God "moving in his majesty and power" (D&C 88:47). "Faith unto repentance" (see Alma 34:15–17) means having sufficient faith for "a change of mind." To have one's mind changed requires an infusion of the truth about Jesus and the doctrines of His kingdom that will restructure one's framework of understanding.

Repentance is helped if we are being assisted not only by the promptings of the Spirit but also by someone who, as a true friend, is willing "to exhort with all long-suffering and doctrine" (2 Timothy 4:2). To exhort isn't simply to scold, though it sometimes may include that; but it involves tender beseeching, entreating, and comforting. The long-suffering prescribed includes not only patience but also forbearance with another while he or she is in the untidy process of trying to set things right. These and other doctrines are needed to help produce such "a change of mind." No wonder the Lord said we, His servants, are to "teach the doctrine[s] of the kingdom" (D&C 88:77), which are especially powerful (see Alma 31:5).

No wonder, too, all of us need to learn some things "by sad experience," such as how to handle power correctly, lest our faith fail. Such lessons are not just for Saul, David, or Thomas B. Marsh.

Obedience training was necessary even for stellar Adam. When asked why he offered sacrifices, he said he didn't know, except that he had been so commanded by the Lord (see Moses 5:5–8). He knew the significance of angelic ministrations. In contrast, like a lot of us, Jonah in effect said, "I'll go where you want me to go, dear Lord—just as long as it's not to a Nineveh!" Then came a whale of a lesson, followed by Jonah's humble pledge: "I will sacrifice unto thee with the voice of thanksgiving; I will pay that that I have vowed. Salvation is of the Lord." (Jonah 2:9.)

We are to "strip" ourselves of both our fears and our jealousies (D&C 67:10), which is part of "putting off the natural man" (see Mosiah 3:19). The verb *strip* suggests a painful peeling off of such fleshly tendencies rather than a gradual erosion, though the latter may still account for one grinding way by which we finally learn "in process of time."

Jealousy also signifies the insecurity of the flesh. The natural man requires constant reassurance. Implicit in jealousy is the erroneous assumption that God is unjust, unnoticing, partial, and a respecter of persons. Once again, understanding of and faith in God's character is so important. The fears of the flesh drive jealousy and can cause us to practice one-upmanship, or to try to manipulate family, friends, and neighbors. If we know and remember who we really are and to whom we really belong, being jealous about our standing among peers is pathetically provincial!

Jealousy also insists that undue importance be given to recognition, credit, applause, and to grabbing one's place in the sun, even though one insensitively elbows others out. Have we forgotten the majesty of Jesus' meekness?

Jealousy brings out the smallness in us, not the saintliness. The mother of James and John worried unnecessarily about who would sit on the left-hand and right-hand sides of Jesus in His kingdom. Saul, swollen with ego, needed to be reminded that there was a time "when thou wast little in thine own sight" (1 Samuel 15:17).

Our "fears," in turn, are dangerous, because they can cause us to worry too much about what might happen to our bodies and not enough about what could happen to our spirits. Our fears can cause us to wonder whether, after all, God will really protect us. These fears reflect a lack of faith in both God's capacity and character, including His love for us. We worry, for example, that we might be hurt or put down because He is inattentive to our needs. Oh, how familiar we all are with such worries!

The surging adrenaline of our "fears" of the flesh can blot

out our spiritual memories. Laman and Lemuel feared what Laban could do. Yet they knew how marvelously God had delivered Moses and his hundreds of thousands of people from Pharaoh and his thousands in the remarkable passage through the Red Sea!

Similarly, our fears can cause us to question God's plan of salvation, even when we know beforehand that there are some things we must either die from, live with, or pass through. Developing sufficient faith enables us to say and to mean, "Let [God] do what seemeth Him good" (1 Samuel 3:18; see also 2:12; D&C 40:3; 100:1). Such submission is a sure sign that the fears of the flesh have been put in their place.

In Lehi's vision of the rod of iron, a most interesting outcome was described. Some Church members, "after they had tasted of the fruit . . . were ashamed" (1 Nephi 8:28). Why? For some objective reason? No. Simply "because of those that were scoffing at them." We see a few around us who simply can't stand to be separated from the "politically correct" multitudes in the great and spacious building. These multitudes are "in the attitude of mocking and pointing their fingers towards those who had come at and were partaking of the fruit" (1 Nephi 8:26–27). The "finger of scorn" has its own way of separating the faithful from those who have little or no faith (see 1 Nephi 8:33).

Like Lehi, the faithful in our time will endure the pointing fingers of scorn from the world and "[heed] them not," even when the ironical fact is that some of those pointing fingers of scorn once grasped the iron rod.

Some have little faith which then fails, because they can't stand the peer pressure, the shame and scorn heaped upon them by the world. They simply cannot learn to "despise the shame of the world" (see 2 Nephi 9:18), and they let go of the iron rod and slip away. Learning to despise the shame of the world means coming to think nothing of it, just as in taking no heed of temptation (see D&C 20:22).

This does not mean that the men and women of Christ have

a bunker mentality—far from it! They are to move about in the world while wearing the whole armor of God and carrying the sturdy shield of faith, with which they will quench the fiery darts of the adversary (see Ephesians 6:16). Since the disciple seeks to share the contagion of his faith, he certainly does not live in isolation. He will have love in his heart, even when the love of many in the world waxes cold (see Matthew 24:12). He will have peace in his soul and his home, even when peace has been taken from the earth. He will be spiritually intact in a churning world in which "all things are in commotion."

The fulfillment of the Lord's prophecy about hastening His work in the last days (see D&C 88:73) will bring a compression as well as a commotion of events (see D&C 88:91). There will also be discouraging things, such as the decibels of discontent emanating from those few who signal they are "on their way out" of the Church. The failure of faith can be a private thing or, as with Sidney Rigdon, a public thing. Of Brother Rigdon's giving up, John Taylor said: "I remember a remark made by Sidney Rigdon—I suppose he did not live his religion—I do not think he did—his knees began to shake in Missouri, and on one occasion he said, 'Brethren, every one of you take your own way, for the work seems as though it had come to an end.' Brigham Young encouraged the people, and Joseph Smith told them to be firm and maintain their integrity, for God would be with his people and deliver them."[18]

Our eventual place in eternity turns on whether our knees bend or shake and what we think and do in daily life.

CHAPTER

7

Faith That Takes Up the Cross Daily

Various divine observations about human nature, such as the one that follows, indicate why developing and sustaining daily faith can be such a challenge: "And thus we see that except the Lord doth chasten his people with many afflictions, yea, except he doth visit them with death and with terror, and with famine and with all manner of pestilence, they will not remember him" (Helaman 12:3).

Why is this so? Is it simply unintended forgetfulness? Or is it a failure of intellectual integrity by our refusing to review and to acknowledge past blessings? Or is it a lack of meekness which requires the repetition of such stern lessons, because we neglect the milder and gentler signs beckoning us to "remember Him"? Deliberately cultivating spiritual memories thus becomes a large part of maintaining daily faith. Counting our blessings is one way of discounting our fears and anxieties.

Keeping a more careful database of the past would certainly make it easier to count our blessings, for surely we truly have "proved [God] in days that are past."[1] Yet even when we are wise enough to count our blessings, we usually do it without weighing them. A numerical inventory, by itself, is not sufficient. Some blessings are of extraordinary size and significance. A harried homemaker who finds a much-needed parking place is briefly grateful for that small blessing, but it scarcely compares to the eternal blessings which can flow from the temple's initiatory ordinances. There is no democracy of blessings; hence counting blessings without weighing them may unintentionally be undervaluing them.

Daily faith helps us endure the seeming repetitiveness of life. As an example, faith permits us to see opportunities for service which might not appear as such to the casual glance or which the unfaithful see as mere repetition. Faith also helps us to endure the repeated lessons of life with gratitude for God's long-suffering, which persists in providing fresh opportunities to overcome our shortcomings. Even though we seem to have been through some of the experiences before, faith permits us to accept what is thus freshly allotted to us along with seeing life's vexations as being "but for a small moment" (D&C 122:4).

John Donne observed that "the memory is oftener the Holy Ghost's pulpit that he preaches in."[2] Memory has also been described as "the stomach of the soul." Memory digests and assimilates the blessings we receive from God. On one occasion, Jesus observed of His disciples that they did "not understand"; furthermore, they did "neither remember" (see Matthew 16:8–10). Remembering and understanding should be daily conceptual companions. We need the Spirit daily to help us remember daily. Otherwise memory lapses will occur when we are most vulnerable. It is not natural to the natural man to remember yesterday's blessings gratefully, especially when today's needs of the flesh press steadily upon him. The Spirit also brings us increased understanding as it teaches us.

In some precious and personal moments there are brief, sudden surges of recognition of an immortal insight, a doctrinal *déjà vu*. These flashes from the mirror of memory can remind us and inspire us, especially in the midst of life's taxing telestial traffic jams, which can otherwise cause us to grow weary and faint in our minds.

The scriptures, of course, constitute our collective memory, without which so many have "suffered in ignorance" (Mosiah 1:3). Searched and "likened" to ourselves effectively, the scriptures can thereby "[enlarge] the memory of this people" (see Alma 37:8), emancipating us from the limitations of our own time and place; the spiritual database is expanded. If we are meek, the case studies in the scriptures help us to see our own case more clearly. In fact, it is the process of likening that results in enlarging.

Hardness of heart first comes in the form of forgetfulness, and one consequence of stiffneckedness is an unwillingness or inability to look back at life's lessons. When an individual or a people can no longer be stirred up to remembrance, they soon become "past feeling" as well (1 Nephi 17:45; Ephesians 4:19; Moroni 9:20).

At the Judgment Day, however, there will be inclusive objectivity. Not only will we have what the Book of Mormon calls "bright recollection" and "perfect remembrance" of our misdeeds, but the joyous things will be brought forward and restored too. We shall know "even as we know now." (Alma 5:18; 11:43; see also D&C 93:33.) We shall see "eye to eye" (Mosiah 12:22; 15:29) because of a shared database.

Among the "all things [that] shall be restored" (Alma 40:23) will be memory, including, eventually, our premortal memories. Consider the joy of our being conjoined in mind and heart by the relevant memories of both the first and the second estates.

What a flood of feeling will come to us then, when a loving God deems it wise that memories be fully restored! This refreshing flood of fact will further increase our gratefulness for how far back God's long-suffering goes and for the lovingkindness of Jesus' voluntary atonement!

Meanwhile, however, we struggle with remembering.

Sometimes, to our regret, it is much as Mary Warnock wrote: "Anything that is over . . . is a lost possession. . . . The past is a paradise from which we are necessarily excluded."[3] The Holy Ghost can help greatly, if we will let Him.

It is clear that even life's deserved reveries do not seem to last very long before being crowded out by the next round of anxieties. Life's reveries and refreshing recesses are brief, at best, hence spiritual memories should be deliberately culti- vated as a matter of our self-interest.

Faith unashamedly uses remembrance as a resource for integrating the past, the present, and the future. Granted, in some circumstances we may not presently "know the mean- ing of all things," but by remembering the past, we certainly can know that God loves us; and therefore we can trust Him now, just as we have proved Him in the past. (See 1 Nephi 11:17.)

Faith is especially needed, however, when there is nothing in our memories to prepare us for something special. Jesus taught the Apostles about the resurrection. Yet it was difficult for them to understand so miraculous a thing—especially something that had never before happened in all of human history: "as yet they knew not the scripture, that he must rise again from the dead" (John 20:9).

It takes faith to enter life's fray every day. In the constant war of the individual spirit against the flesh, it is so easy to settle for a losing accommodation with the flesh. We don't pay enough attention to Jesus' commandment about denying our- selves *and* taking up the cross *daily* (see Luke 9:23). Taking up the cross daily is an affirmation of the meaning of life, even if we log only a few miles a day in the journey of discipleship. Each increment not only moves us along but also, what is very important, maintains the desired direction. The lack of daily affirmation, on the other hand, such as through service, prayer, and forgiveness, can be a perilous pause. Resuming the journey after any pause is not automatic. Every delay risks the difficulty of resumption.

Comparing the word of God to a seed, as Alma does, underscores the need for us to give regular place in our lives for planting that precious seed. We do this by regularly providing both the desire and the time to search and ponder by connecting the word (the doctrines of the kingdom) to daily life. Doing so enlarges one's soul, enlightens one's understanding, and increases one's faith. (See Alma 32:28–29.)

Desire, or even a particle of faith, can be enough initially to cause us to thus "give place" for planting gospel doctrines—"the word"—in our lives and nurturing the doctrines thereafter. The failure to do these simple basic things—planting and nurturing—underlies the subsequent failures of faith, whether in the failure to pay tithing, to pray, to understand personal trials, or to build a better marriage, and so forth.

The members' faith in the Brethren as living Apostles and prophets not only provides the needed direction but also clearly sustains those leaders in their arduous chores. There is more to it than this, however. Sustaining them also means that we realize those select men are conscious of their own imperfections; each is even grateful that the other Brethren have strengths and talents he may not have. The gratitude of the Brethren for being so sustained thus includes appreciation for members' willingness to overlook the imperfections of the overseers. The faithful realize the Apostles are working out their salvation, too, including the further development of the Christlike virtues. Serious discipleship requires us all to be "on the way to perfection" rather than thinking we are already in the arrival lounge.

Lorenzo Snow said of the Prophet Joseph Smith's minor imperfections that he marveled how the Lord could use him, anyway, even with those imperfections. This gave Lorenzo Snow hope that the Lord might be able to use him, too, even with his imperfections.

However, even with the awareness of the imperfections in each other, we should not let our own weaknesses go unchallenged or unremoved, even though we need time and long-suffering in which to eliminate these weaknesses or to make them into strengths.

Since faith is markedly increased by "the word," it is vital to use every opportunity to hear or read "the word" regularly, even daily, if possible. Brigham Young hungered for the word in his early discipleship. While he was not easily impressed by anyone, his regard for Joseph was deep, and it never left him. Of this prophet-pupil relationship, Brigham, now himself the prophet, said: "An angel never watched [Joseph] closer than I did, and that is what has given me the knowledge I have today. I treasure it up, and ask the Father in the name of Jesus, to help my memory when information is wanted."[4]

How blessed we in succeeding generations have been that Brigham listened so carefully to Joseph! Brigham's harvest became our harvest. Someday perhaps we shall learn, too, how the Prophet gained reciprocally from his faithful friend and pupil, Brigham.

Our desires matter greatly. The linkage between our desires and our deeds is so clear. "For I, the Lord, will judge all men according to their works, according to the desire of their hearts" (D&C 137:9).

If our desires are strong and righteous, they can move us to the needed daily actions (see Alma 32). Abraham is a classic case. He genuinely desired greater happiness. He thus desired to have the priesthood blessings his fathers had once had, even though his home environment apparently was bad. Abraham let those desires work in him until the day came when faith moved him away to start a different life. He certainly "gave place" by giving up his status quo in order to establish the better life he desired in "another place of residence." (See Abraham 1:1–2.) His sights were really set on the City of God, for he desired a heavenly country (see Hebrews 11:10, 16).

Abraham didn't start off fully developed, however. He was required to go through various and trying developmental experiences. Abraham finally acquired full spiritual submissiveness, as exemplified by his doing as bidden even in that testing moment when he did not know there would be a ram in the thicket!

Abraham was helped by being able to see "the promises" that were "afar off." He was "persuaded of them, and embraced them." (Hebrews 11:13.) He was clear about his desires. Similarly, those who have a grasp of the plan of salvation today understand what lies ahead, "afar off." Meanwhile they regard themselves as "pilgrims on the earth" (Hebrews 11:13). If, however, a person lacks the adornment of Christian virtues, declared Peter, he "cannot see afar off" (2 Peter 1:9).

Desire, therefore, plays such a leading part in building faith by means of which we see with the eye of faith.

Righteous desires may be a personally initiated yearning which cannot be supplied from outside oneself. But if there is a spark of desire in us, we can let that desire work sufficiently until we "give place" by planting "the word" in our lives, thoughts, and schedules. Besides, keeping our gaze on the better things which are "afar off" is helpful when the present is so difficult and when we need chastisements as correctives because we are veering off course.

Life has a way of offering almost daily lessons to us, if we are meek enough to learn. Brigham Young said, "When chastisements come, let them be what they may, let us always be willing and ready to kiss the rod, and reverence the hand that administers it, acknowledging the hand of God in all things."[5]

Yet how hard it is on occasion to submit, especially amid the ambiguity and the checkered circumstances of daily life.[6]

Submissiveness has another benefit; it will cut down on our verbalism. Many of us do what Jesus never did: we talk too much. This is risky for several reasons, one of which Brigham Young identified, saying, "You cannot hide the heart, when the mouth is open."[7] Fortunately, those who are becoming men and women of Christ are improving and need not fear if their hearts are seen.

Meekness is a great blessing, whether shown in receiving

correction or in avoiding the multiplying of words. Those of us who multiply words are usually displaying a desire for more "air time." The meek are more settled in their views; they can be succinct without feeling unappreciated. They can even let someone else say what they would have said, and still not feel left out.

Sometimes we are offended because, though we already know we have made a mistake, we resent its being pointed out by others, especially publicly. Or we get miffed when we are visibly ineffective, especially while others seem to be "scoring points." We are like some athletes who, seeing a game slipping away, in their frustration begin to commit flagrant fouls or act out their disappointment in other visible ways.

It takes daily faith to keep a check on one's enflamed ego or to regroup after losing control. Not many days pass without a challenge to one's ego—perhaps only hours lie between such tests.

Travel on the straight and narrow path is made much easier if we are putting off more and more of the heavy and onerous burdens of the ego-saturated and jealous natural man.

Each event in our daily lives, however seemingly small, is part of a scattergram of responses with a discernable pattern. The failure of faith, therefore, does not usually occur with the placing of only one particular dot or episode on the scattergram. The pattern is subtly cumulative, as momentum shifts toward or away from faith in our choice of actions in daily life.

There are so many little, focusing moments in which the reflexes of faith are either in place or they are not. Defining moments are preceded by preparatory moments. If previously we have behaved properly, though tempted, or if we have been gentle, though irritated, and if we have reached out to help others, though beset with personal problems, as we meet the defining moments these reflexes will steady us. Reflexes do not introduce new and sudden surges. Rather, they represent the harvest of what has passed. How good, for instance, are we at receiving bad news? If we have buckled in the past, that is one thing; but if we have absorbed bad news and moved on, we are likely to be able to gird up our loins again. If we have hedged instead of trusted in the Lord, then we are likely to hedge again. Equivocation followed by equivocation can become its own destination.

An especially helpful boost to daily discipleship is achieving the regular remission of our sins. Reinforcing blessings accompany that vital process; "the remission of sins bringeth meekness, and lowliness of heart; and because of meekness and lowliness of heart cometh the visitation of the Holy Ghost, which Comforter filleth with hope and perfect love" (Moroni 8:26).

The high personal yield continues as perfect love, in turn, "casteth out fear: because fear hath torment. He that feareth is not made perfect in love." (1 John 4:18.)

How wonderful to be filled with love in a time when "the love of many [waxes] cold" (Matthew 24:12) and to be free of fear even as men's hearts fail them "for fear"! (Luke 21:26.)

Maintaining developmental balance on the straight and narrow path, however, requires orthodoxy in thought and behavior. After all, human happiness is at stake, because orthodoxy represents felicity and safety! Daily faith brings the blessings of orthodoxy. G. K. Chesterton wrote of "huge blunders" in human happiness caused by the lack of daily spiritual balance, saying "There never was anything so perilous or so exciting as orthodoxy."[8]

Orthodoxy requires balancing all the gospel's correct principles—not only justice and mercy—in our daily behavior. Gospel principles in action require the matchless synchronization of the Spirit, which is why the gift of the Holy Ghost is such a great gift! We rightly sing the words, "more used would I be," but those pleading words can best be said if we are guided by the Holy Ghost.

The doctrines of the restored gospel of Jesus Christ are very powerful. If they are pulled apart from each other and isolated, they cannot function fully or properly. Hence the doctrines of the Church need each other just as much as the people of the Church need each other. Errors in doctrine produce behavioral excesses which, in turn, produce great unhappiness. It takes daily faith to achieve daily balance.

Even love, if not checked by the seventh commandment, can be wholly carnal. Even the laudable emphasis upon loyalty to the family still has to be checked by the first great commandment, lest one, for example, be more loyal to an errant family than to God.

The full gospel of Jesus Christ is greater than any of its parts. It is larger than any of its programs or principles.

Jesus said balance is even needed in our renderings as between God and Caesar (see Matthew 22:21). Balance is needed, too, between simultaneously feeding the flock and keeping wolves out of the flock.

Even patience is to be balanced with reproving "betimes with sharpness, when moved upon by the Holy Ghost" (D&C 121:43), *betimes* meaning early, or soon.

Sometimes in daily life our eyes are "holden" (see Luke 24:16). Things to which we are so close and which should be obvious enough are, ironically, often unclear to us. We can't always make out what lies just two steps ahead. Instead, we are to trust the Lord and walk by faith in such circumstances, taking the next first step, until the wisdom of the Lord indicates otherwise. Later we will see how we stared directly at the obvious but still could not see it. Besides, having received so many blessings involving one divine "yes" after another, we should not be surprised if there is an occasional, divine "no," if only because of divine timing.

If everything in one's immediate context were constantly clear, God's plan would not work. Hard choices as well as passing through periodic mists of darkness are needed in order to maintain life's basic reality—that we are to overcome by faith.

Literally, a person's space and circumstance—the locus of his life—form his own individual classroom. It is in those personal classrooms—the only ones readily available to the Teacher—that we are given our chances to learn the Lord's lessons. These classrooms constitute our individual fields of action. Hence the ironies we experience seem so personal, perhaps even undeserved, because they occur on our own turf, making some lessons especially public and painful.

If we are meek, each of us will be taught in whatever constitutes his own classroom, into which life's daily episodes are poured.

Why is it sometimes necessary to live daily with a "thorn in the flesh"? Paul said in his case it helped him not be "exalted above measure" because of all his spiritual blessings (2 Corinthians 12:7). This insight applies to more of us than Paul, who had the faith to introspect, to plead, and then to trust God with regard to living with his undisclosed vexation.

Daily faith is surely needed when a particular challenge is to be resolved. The challenge may be either a "live with" (it isn't going to go away) or a "pass-through" situation challenge (intense, "but for a small moment").

In what finally turn out to be the "live with" situations, it is only as one's importuning ends that his "live with" can really begin. This is part of becoming "alive in Christ because of our faith" (2 Nephi 25:25–26). It is only in daily life that we become "dead indeed unto sin" by becoming "alive unto God through Jesus Christ our Lord" (Romans 6:11).

No wonder that, reinforcingly and repeatedly, we are counseled to talk of, rejoice in, preach of, and prophecy of Christ. Why? So that we and "our children may know to what source they may look for a remission of their sins." (See 2 Nephi 25:26.) Remission brings justified hope, which thereafter companies with faith and charity. Looking to Christ—including looking to His atonement and character—requires our talking and rejoicing over these realities.

Though we rightly speak of "faith and works," faith by itself, as has been shown, is constant work! It is a work to be done and a process best pursued while being not only "anxiously engaged" but also engaged with "fear and trembling." Otherwise we may lose our concentration on Christ.

Another daily need is for us to give place in our lives by making room for others to work through their imperfections—just as we need room when working through ours. There is a special need for us to be understanding and long-suffering in those trying circumstances with others who are going through their own necessary spiritual calisthenics. Our faith and patience are thus called upon daily.

So it is that bearing one another's burdens in daily life consists not only in carrying the physical burdens or helping out in the obvious ways but also by bearing one another's burdens as we "put up" with each other's imperfections—repeatedly and frustratingly! As we witness, firsthand, the soul-struggles of others to develop a particular virtue, we can see how vital it is that we be more filled with loving-kindness and long-suffering. We then understand, better than ever before, what Jesus meant when he said, "Take my yoke upon you, and learn of me" (Matthew 11:29). Longitudinal learning requires long-suffering.

Whether we realize or acknowledge it, each of our daily mortal acts "has a tendency . . . either for good or evil."[9] Life is incremental. What we do in seemingly small moments or at particular points on the path, in process of time brings large consequences—good and bad. "In a given moment," Brigham Young said ". . . there is but a hair's breadth between the depths of infidelity and the heights of . . . faith."[10] Small moments and small decisions tilt the soul. For instance, inner resentments and unexpressed murmurings can finally take their toll. When these are being acted out as doubt deepens, Brigham warned, "it will not be a great while before you begin to neglect your prayers, refuse to pay your tithing, and find fault with the authorities of the Church."[11]

Just as miracles do not sustain faith by themselves, they

do not automatically see us through trials, either. Daily faith is what sees us through.

The histories of the Three Witnesses so attest. Orson Pratt said in this regard: "This should be a lesson to the Latter-day Saints, that when we do see some small miracles wrought, we should strive to strengthen ourselves up in the spirit of our religion, with light and knowledge and information—to gain all that we possibly can, that we may be spiritually strengthened; a miracle is external to the senses, and has only an exciting effect upon the mind. Unless it is accompanied by the Spirit of the living God in the heart, what are we benefited?"[12] Laman and Lemuel experienced at various times such an "exciting effect" upon their minds, but they did not develop lasting faith.

Even though Lehi taught Laman and Lemuel "many great things," and even though they had seen the Lord's hand do remarkable things, still, in daily life, these two were not sufficiently interested to inquire of the Lord, or to "look unto the Lord as they ought" (1 Nephi 15:3).[13] In comparison, Nephi's faith not only regularly caused him to "look unto [his] God" but also aided him, so that in difficult daily life he "did not murmur against the Lord because of [his] afflictions" (1 Nephi 18:16). Like Abel,[14] Nephi clearly understood the daily implications of the stretching plan of salvation and also the role of personal afflictions therein. Laman and Lemuel, shorn of the plan's perspectives, "just didn't get it!"

Having daily access to the Spirit, therefore, is better than periodic miracles.

There are other things we can do daily to bolster the faith of others as well as our own. Peter prescribed: "But sanctify the Lord God in your hearts: and be ready always to give an answer to every man that asketh you a reason of the hope that is in you with meekness and fear" (1 Peter 3:15).

The word *answer* here means a verbal defense or a reason statement. The very act of so giving our witness will help not only others but also ourselves. As Brigham Young said, we will grow in the knowledge of the truth as we "impart knowledge to others," by means of which we "will also grow and increase." Hence, President Young continued, "Wherever you see an opportunity to do good, do it, for that is the way to increase and grow in the knowledge of the truth." If, instead, we are reluctant to do good, we "will become contracted" in our views and feelings.[15]

As we progress, we can come to have "an actual knowledge that the course of life which [one] is pursuing is according to [God's] will."[16] No wonder Paul wrote of Enoch that "before his translation he had this testimony, that he pleased God" (Hebrews 11:5). This is not to say that such a person's life at any moment is finally finished, complete, or perfect. Rather, it is that the fundamental, daily direction of one's life, even in the midst of one's afflictions and inadequacies, is basically approved. So we are to continue the journey and endure to the end, utilizing daily faith. Faith can seldom rest, therefore. It is called upon just as soon as one's next irritation, temptation, or affliction appears.

Each temptation is real, but so is faith in one's identity. Each affliction is to some degree tormenting, but the plan of salvation reassures us about ourselves and outcomes. An irritation will be keenly felt, but it can be overcome by seeing the irritation for what it often is—including seeing it as an extrusion of yet untamed ego!

With faith, as did Joseph anciently under serious temptation, one can self-interrogate: "How . . . can I do this great wickedness, and sin against God?" Joseph knew his own identity and the responsibility it carried. He went further, however, even reminding his temptress of her own identity and responsibility, noting that her husband "hath [not] kept back anything from me but thee, because thou art his wife." (See Genesis 39:7–20.) The natural man, however, does not put such relevant questions to himself.

Neglecting our prayers, tithes, and attendance at essential Church meetings is a failure not only of faith but also of patience and meekness. It is like saying, "Lord, I believe, but I am above and beyond such small duties"; or, "I've had my turn." In contrast, the character of the Redeemer of the world is such that though He had no sins to be remitted, He humbly condescended to be baptized and "showeth unto the children of men that . . . he humbleth himself before the Father . . . that he would be obedient . . . in keeping his commandments" (2 Nephi 31:7–9; see also 1 Nephi 11:26–27).

Even if one is in general compliance, irritability over doing the "daily things" betrays a lack of patience and meekness. We may even be willing to go through the motions of discipleship but, erroneously, feel we need not be especially pleasant while so doing. One looks in vain for irritability on Jesus' part, as He worked out the great atonement in the midst of awful aloneness and of a lack of appreciation for what He was accomplishing.

Do we really think that Jesus' central attribute—loving-kindness—is one from which we are developmentally exempt? Is not loving-kindness the very lubricant needed in so many daily human interactions, lest selfish and contagious irritability carry the day? Does not meekness mean at least holding back one's own ego (the only one we can control, after all) from the congested daily collisions of so many other egos in the midst of life's fray? Sensitive and defensive driving protects riders in both cars when a foot is removed from the accelerator of ego.

Irritability indicates that one feels imposed upon. It suggests we were expecting to be insulated from irritations amid our important tasks; or that we are not "content with the things which the Lord hath allotted unto [us]" (Alma 29:3); or that, even if we do not question the fairness of the allocations, we may wonder whether the Lord's grace really is sufficient for the meek. Most of us resent having our weaknesses worked on. Yet how else can the weakness eventually be replaced by a strength? (See Ether 12:26–27.)

Even so, a person already knows too well that the gap

between what he is and what he should be is large. Why the constant reminders? Why the incessant demands? Can't one rest a little while longer before starting a quiet new campaign of self-improvement? No, because being "valiant" in our testimony of Jesus includes precious few recesses and no vacations! (See D&C 76:79.) The school day in the mortal classroom is so very brief at best. Remember Jacob's seven years of labor to win Rachel, which seemed but a few days because of his love for her? (See Genesis 29:20.)

Thus we come back, again and again, to the need for daily faith in God's plan of salvation and in His capacity to accomplish His planned work, including His work with us (see 2 Nephi 27:20–21).

Of course, we can settle for being "honorable"—no small designation. We can forego receiving "the fulness of the Father." But it means a moon versus sun difference in the firmaments of our future lives (see D&C 76:71–75). It is the natural man who is always ready to give away his future for today's mess of pottage. As Latter-day Saints we need to be ever mindful that what lies ahead—all the "thrones and dominions, principalities and powers"—are to be "set forth upon all who have endured valiantly for the gospel of Christ" (D&C 1:21–29).

Meanwhile, however, daily life can be so hectic. The weariness as well as the weakness of the flesh can press us down. A child's milk is spilled when a young mother is already late for an appointment to do good. A fan belt breaks on a home teacher's car on his way to visit the sick. Or try getting an extended family together for a temple session, and behold the many intrusions and frustrations! These frustrating, unscheduled intrusions, while only momentary, nevertheless irritate our faith and patience.

God knows our predicament, and if we know He has love and plans for us, we can better cope. Meanwhile, however, we should impose what added "wisdom and order" we can upon our hectic circumstances. It takes faith to make the specific choices needed to meet the "wisdom and order" and "strength and means" tests. (D&C 10:4; Mosiah 4:27.)

There are wise limits in daily life. For instance, how many of the various "lessons" for their children can young parents sustain, financially as well as transportationally? How much such "good" can their children actually stand? We sometimes do so much *for* our children that we can do nothing *with* them!

The architecture of the plan of salvation sets forth the macro things, but with these come implied tactical, ordering priorities. A lack of faith in the overall plan's priorities can induce unnecessary tactical hecticness.

If, for instance, we seek to teach the rising generation how "sacrifice brings forth the blessings of heaven," can this be done without their experiencing measured sacrifice? Can the Fall—with the resultant necessity of work "by the sweat of the brow"—be taught without the youth having validating experiences with work? The latter is hard to achieve, especially for some advantaged youth in some urban settings. But we ignore the principle of work at our developmental peril.

Wise parents, by planning to ensure experience with appropriate work and sacrifice, are utilizing their faith to help their children—even if a few designated chores go against the grain of what their peers are required to do. The Lord's grace will be sufficient for striving young parents who wish to be anxiously but not hectically engaged.

The home is usually the place where most of our faith is established and increased, for there we witness the examples of righteous parents as we work out our salvation in a setting that requires love, forgiveness, patience, and all the other virtues. How sad, therefore, that some homes are merely a pit stop, when they should be a prep school for the celestial kingdom.

Amid the frustrations at having done what is right only to see things go wrong, faith is taxed unless it is augmented by patience. We often need to wait for better perspective than the present provides. Then, as the darkness of disappointment yields to the dawn's light, purposes previously hidden become apparent. However, if in our frustrations we "rush to judgment" by being upset or angry, we let loose a flood of toxic emotions. The workhorse virtues of faith and patience can prevent, dilute, dissolve, as well as "mop up" after such toxic floods of feelings.

Our own disappointments can be keen and sharply felt nudges to move us away from a less preferred direction, if we have faith enough to follow the "nudge" instead of griping and railing at these tactical frustrations. Complying with a slothful heart cancels out much of the gain, because then our obedience is outward only. The whole soul has not been moved. Slothful compliance is cousin to compelled compliance! (See D&C 58:26.) Whether the compliance is slack or sluggish, the lesson of the experience has largely been lost.

Disappointments can also be blessings in disguise. This is especially so when we envy those who got what we have wanted. The sailors on the port-bound U.S.S. *Enterprise* were slowed by heavy seas and a malfunctioning escort destroyer, the U.S.S. *Dunlap*. Hence the *Enterprise* would not make Pearl Harbor, after all, as scheduled, for the weekend of December 7, 1941. Eighteen planes, however, were permitted to take off and proceed to Hawaii. Some left behind must have envied those "lucky" pilots! However, those unfortunate planes arrived during the attack of Pearl Harbor, and six were shot down.[17] Envy is usually as uninformed as it is insistent.

Because there cannot be immunities from disappointments, how we handle them is a reflection of how much daily faith we have in Heavenly Father's plan of salvation. Besides, how can we possibly take Jesus' yoke upon us and learn of Him without experiencing what it is like, for example, to do good with good motives, only to have others respond badly and unappreciatively?

Since His course is one loving, patient "eternal round," how can we truly be more like God if we are not willing to take up the cross "daily"? Gaining experience in patient persistence means appreciating, all the more, the character of God and Jesus with their perfect love, long-suffering, and patience!

Quite understandably, faithful Latter-day Saints focus on those dimensions of faith which tell us to "be of good cheer" in the midst of adversity, and on the reality that life is full of joy but also contains trials. We can, unintentionally, miss the opportunity to make faith be life affirming. True, there is "an opposition in all things" (2 Nephi 2:11) in Heavenly Father's plan of salvation. True, there are ambiguities through which we must pass. Life is so designed that caring about necessities and experiencing attendant anxieties do cause the brow to sweat. Additionally, the flesh gives us weaknesses and fears, as already noted.

Even so, life is full of so many wonderful and beautiful things. These we are to appreciate while we endure other things. God, who has given us so much, desires that we develop our capacity to appreciate further the beautiful scenery, the gorgeous sunsets, and a rich earth which has resources and beauties "enough and to spare" (D&C 104:17), though mortal systems may contradict and interdict that abundance. Even so, few lives, indeed, are so barren or so incessantly beset that there is not cause to appreciate and to enjoy all that is lovely and praiseworthy. Part of worshipping God is to appreciate the blessed and happy things even as we pass through the noxious and obnoxious things. True, life's recesses and reveries do not last for long, but they are there, as a foretaste. The many blessings to be counted far outnumber the trials which press upon us.

There are so many reasons, therefore, to open ourselves up to greater appreciation, enabling the soul to expand without hypocrisy and the mind to be enlightened. Our posture on the straight and narrow path is not to be one of resigned, rounded shoulders accompanied by downcast eyes.

God's invitation to "come home" and Jesus' to "come, follow me" are not invitations to a contraction of one's soul; rather they are invitations to expansion and enrichment in both the here and now and the there and then.

The fulness of the Father means just that. His fulness is "all that He hath" (see D&C 84:38). There isn't any more!

As this book comes to an end, I turn again to President Brigham Young, whose wisdom with regard to salvational matters is yet to be fully appreciated by the Church. True, Brigham was the remarkable colonizer of the Great Basin, but if we will ponder his words pertaining to salvation he can be a great colonizer of disciples by helping to form spiritual settlements in the minds of the Saints. Brigham observed that we understand only in part "why we are required to pass through those various incidents of life." Yet, "there is not a single condition of life [and] . . . not one hour's experience but what is beneficial to all those who make it their study, and aim to improve upon the experience they gain."

No wonder daily faith is so important if we are to be constant beneficiaries of the mortal experience. Granted, we have different bearing capacities and different developmental needs, as when "what becomes a trial to one person is not noticed by another."[18] But we have dominion over our own discipleship, and if, indeed, we will make it our "aim" to utilize the "experiences" we have, whether daily or hourly, we can let varied circumstances surge!

Hence, the plea "Lord, increase our faith" is not something He alone can grant. We are coparticipants with Him in a process that is lifelong—and longer.

No wonder God wants us to be "anxiously engaged" now in order to be happily capacitated then to receive His all!

Notes

Introduction

1. *JD* 13:56.

2. F. W. Farrar, *The Life and Work of St. Paul* (London: Cassell and Company, Ltd., 1891), p. 115.

3. Penelope Fitzgerald, *The Knox Brothers* (New York: Coward, McCann & Geoghegan, Inc., 1977), pp. 106–7.

4. *JD* 7:55.

5. See *JD* 13:56.

Chapter 1: Faith in Jesus' Name and Atonement

1. It is significant that the Prophet Joseph rendered "from faith to faith," Paul's words in the King James Version, as "through faith on his name" (JST, Romans 1:17).

2. *JD* 24:34.

3. *JD* 21:26, italics added.

4. *JD* 3:206.

5. Bruce C. Hafen, *The Broken Heart* (Salt Lake City: Deseret Book Company, 1989), p. 20.

6. Stephen E. Robinson, "Believing Christ," *Ensign*, April 1992, pp. 6, 7, 9.

Chapter 2: Faith in Jesus' Character

1. Joseph Smith, *Teachings of the Prophet Joseph Smith,* comp. Joseph Fielding Smith (Salt Lake City: Deseret Book Company, 1976), p. 220. Hereafter cited as *Teachings*.

2. This example of Book of Mormon imagery apparently stuck with President Brigham Young, who later counseled us that "wherever the wisdom of God directs, let our affections

and the labour of our lives be centered to that point, and not set our hearts on going east or west, north or south, on living here or there, on possessing this or that; but let our will be swallowed up in the will of God, allowing him to rule supremely within us until the spirit overcomes the flesh" (*JD* 9:106). On another occasion he said: "The same principle will embrace what is called sanctification. When the will, passions, and feelings of a person are perfectly submissive to God and His requirements, that person is sanctified. It is for my will to be swallowed up in the will of God, that will lead me into all good, and crown me ultimately with immortality and eternal lives." (*JD* 2:123.)

3. *JD* 7:198–99.

4. See E. R. Dodds, *Pagan and Christian in an Age of Anxiety* (New York: W. W. Norton and Co., 1965), pp. 14, 30.

5. Dodds, p. 119.

6. Will Durant, *Caesar and Christ* (New York: Simon and Schuster, 1944), p. 595.

7. See Stephen E. Robinson, "Warring Against the Saints of God," *Ensign,* January 1988, p. 39.

8. *JD* 24:197–98.

9. *Teachings,* p. 113.

10. *JD* 12:170.

11. *Teachings,* p. 343.

12. *JD* 12:81.

13. *JD* 20:190.

Chapter 3: Faith in the Father's Plan of Salvation

1. Alan Hayward, *God Is* (New York: Thomas Nelson, 1978), p. 134.

2. Morris L. West, *The Tower of Babel* (New York: William Morrow and Company, Inc., 1968), p. 183.

3. *JD* 8:115.

4. *JD* 3:336.

5. *Teachings*, p. 220.

6. *Residue* here means the remainder or remnant of the people, those not ministered to by angels, suggesting that real faith is lacking in most, that the people "harden their hearts, all save it were the most believing part of them" (Helaman 16:15).

7. *JD* 9:279.

8. *JD* 1:116.

9. *JD* 8:292.

10. Joseph F. Smith, *Gospel Doctrine* (Salt Lake City: Deseret Book Company, 1939), p. 56.

11. *JD* 10:119–20, italics added.

12. *Abraham Lincoln: A Documentary Portrait Through His Speeches and Writings,* ed. Don E. Fehrenbacher (New York: The New American Library, 1964), p. 41.

13. See *Teachings,* p. 220. See also D&C 130:7.

14. *Teachings,* p. 216.

15. See J. B. Bury et al., *A History of Greece to the Death of Alexander the Great* (New York: The Modern Library, 1913), pp. 263–64.

16. *JD* 26:28.

17. *JD* 17:71.

18. *JD* 7:275.

19. *JD* 26:367.

20. *JD* 23:328.

21. *JD* 21:214–15.

Chapter 4: Faith in the Book of Mormon

1. "The Book of Mormon—Keystone of Our Religion," *Ensign,* November 1986, p. 5.

2. See *Encyclopedia of Mormonism,* 5 vols., ed. Daniel H. Ludlow (New York: Macmillan Publishing Company, 1992), 1:195–201.

3. C. E. M. Joad, *Guide to Philosophy* (New York: Dover Publications, 1946), p. 525.

4. Richard Neitzel Holzapfel and Jeni Broberg Holzapfel, *Women of Nauvoo* (Salt Lake City: Bookcraft, 1992), p. 10.

5. See *Encyclopedia of Mormonism* 1:175.

6. Memorandum made by John H. Gilbert, Esq., September 8, 1892, Palmyra, N.Y.

7. See *Encyclopedia of Mormonism* 1:175.

8. The Reverend Solomon Spaulding, The "Manuscript Found," *Manuscript Story* (Salt Lake City: The Deseret News Company, 1886), p. 66. Spelling and punctuation as in original source. See also *Encyclopedia of Mormonism* 3:1402.

9. Ethan Smith's object was "to show that the natives of America are the descendants of the ten tribes of Israel" (Ethan Smith, *View of the Hebrews,* 2d. ed. [Poultney, Vermont: Smith and Shute, 1825], p. 83). The Book of Mormon is not a record of the ten tribes. Ethan maintains that "the natives of our continent . . . found their way hither . . . over Beerings's [sic] Straits from the north east of Asia" (p. 168). The children of Lehi journeyed from the Middle East to the New World by ship, the Jaredites in barges. Ethan's book is an argument for his thesis. The Book of Mormon is another testament of Jesus Christ, which objective Ethan does not have. (See *Encyclopedia of Mormonism* 4:1509–10.)

10. Ethan Smith, *View of the Hebrews.*

11. *History of the Church* 1:220.

12. "About the Book of Mormon," *Deseret Evening News,* 25 March 1884.

13. *Millennial Star,* 6 February 1882, pp. 86–87.

14. *BYU Studies,* Autumn 1976, p. 35. See also *Encyclopedia of Mormonism* 1:210–12.

15. "Mormonites," *Evangelical Magazine and Gospel Advocate,* 9 April 1831.

16. See Stephen D. Ricks, "Joseph Smith's Means and Methods of Translating the Book of Mormon," and John W. Welch and Tim Rathbone, "The Translation of the Book of Mormon: Basic Historical Information" (Provo: Foundation for Ancient Research and Mormon Studies [F.A.R.M.S.]), 1986.

17. See *Millennial Star* 36 (1874), pp. 498–99.

18. *Ensign*, January 1988, pp. 46–47.

19. John W. Welch, ed. *Reexploring the Book of Mormon* (Salt Lake City: Deseret Book Company, 1992), p. 3.

20. "Insights: An Ancient Window," F.A.R.M.S. Newsletter, February 1986, p. 1.

21. "Last Testimony of Sister Emma," *Saints' Herald,* 1 October 1879, p. 290.

22. Welch and Rathbone, "The Translation of the Book of Mormon: Basic Historical Information," F.A.R.M.S., Preliminary Report, W&R–86, p. 25.

23. "Last Testimony of Sister Emma," p. 289.

24. See *Saints' Herald,* 21 June 1884, p. 396.

25. The list includes Emma Smith, Martin Harris, Oliver Cowdery, David Whitmer, William Smith, Lucy Mack Smith, and Elizabeth Cowdery Johnson; and possibly Michael Morse, Sarah Hellor Conrad, Isaac Hale, Reuben Hale, and Joseph Knight, Sr.

26. "Last Testimony of Sister Emma," pp. 289–90.

27. *Times and Seasons* 3 (15 October 1842):943.

28. As quoted in Joseph Fielding Smith, *Essentials in Church History* (Salt Lake City: Deseret Book Company, 1967), p. 386.

29. Letter of Phineas Young to Brigham Young, 25 April 1850, Church Archives.

30. Autobiography of Bathsheba W. Smith, Church Archives.

31. Letter of Lucy Cowdery Young to Brigham Young, 7 March 1887, Church Archives.

32. See *Encyclopedia of Mormonism* 1:211.

33. See Matthias F. Cowley, *Wilford Woodruff* (Salt Lake City: Bookcraft, 1970), p. 68.

34. See *History of the Church* 6:317.

35. *Teachings,* p. 368.

36. *The Personal Writings of Joseph Smith,* ed. Dean C. Jesse (Salt Lake City, Deseret Book Company, 1984), p. 395.

37. *Hymns,* 1985, no. 27.

Chapter 5: Faith in Gospel Ordinances

1. *The Words of Joseph Smith,* Andrew F. Ehat and Lyndon W. Cook, eds. (Provo, Utah: Religious Studies Center, Brigham Young University, 1980), p. 213.

2. *JD* 12:99.

3. *JD* 9:329–30.

4. *JD* 2:3.

5. *Teachings,* p. 324.

6. *JD* 25:197–98.

7. *JD* 13:280.

8. *The Words of Joseph Smith,* p. 120.

9. Bruce R. McConkie, comp., *Doctrines of Salvation,* 3 vols. (Salt Lake City: Bookcraft, 1954–56), 2:165.

10. *A Mind Awake: An Anthology of C. S. Lewis,* Clyde S. Kilby, ed. (New York: Harcourt Brace Jovanovich, Publishers, 1968), p. 23.

11. *Scientific American,* February 1990, p. 19.

12. David L. Chandler, "Largest Structure Found in Universe Defies Explanation," *Sacramento Union,* 19 November 1989, p. 22.

13. Chaisson and McMillan, *Astronomy Today* (New York: Prentice Hall, 1993), p. 559.

14. Stephen Strass, *Globe and Mail,* 5 February 1990, p. A2.

15. F. Dyson, as quoted in Barrow and Tibler, *The Anthropic Cosmological Principle* (New York: Clarendon Press, 1986), foreword page.

Chapter 6: Faith That Fails Not

1. *JD* 2:257.

2. *JD* 1:123.

3. *JD* 4:131, 134.

4. *JD* 2:256.

5. *JD* 2:257.

6. Ivan Illich, in *Oxford Dictionary of Quotations* (Oxford: Oxford University Press, 1980), p. 270.

7. *JD* 1:315.

8. Cowper, in *Oxford Dictionary of Quotations,* p. 166.

9. *Oxford Quotations,* p. 165.

10. *JD* 2:256.

11. *JD* 3:247.

12. *The Quotable Lewis,* Walter Martindale and Jerry Root, eds. (Wheaton, Illinois: Tyndale House Publishers, Inc., 1989), p. 211.

13. *JD* 8:16.

14. *Teachings,* p. 146.

15. *JD* 21:268–69.

16. *JD* 5:83.

17. *JD* 17:199–200.

18. *JD* 11:25–26.

Chapter 7: Faith That Takes Up the Cross Daily

1. *Hymns,* no. 19.

2. *Donne's Prebend Sermons,* Janel M. Mueller, ed. (Cambridge, Massachusetts: Harvard University Press, 1971), p. 33.

3. Mary Warnock, *Memory* (London: Faber and Faber, 1987), p. 77.

4. Brigham Young's remarks at semiannual general conference 8 October 1866, as reported by G. D. Watt. (Church Archives.) On another occasion, Brigham elaborated: "In my experience I never did let an opportunity pass of getting with the Prophet Joseph and of hearing him speak in public or in private, so that I might draw understanding from the fountain from which he spoke, that I might have it and bring it forth when it was needed. . . . In the days of the Prophet Joseph, such moments were more precious to me than all the wealth of the world. No matter how great my poverty—if I had to borrow meal to feed my wife and children, I never let an opportunity pass of learning what the Prophet had to impart." (*JD* 12:269–70.)

5. *JD* 2:280.

6. Elder Wilford Woodruff's counsel is parallel to Brigham's

and highly relevant today: "When I am out of the way, and when you are out of the way, I thank God that we have a man to preside over us, who loves us enough to chastise us; it is for our good, and I believe we have been always ready to receive the chastening rod from our superiors when they thought fit to give it to us, and kiss the rod that chastened us" (*JD* 2:198).

7. *JD* 6:74. See also James 1:26; 3:5–6.

8. G. K. Chesterton, *Orthodoxy* (Garden City, New York: Doubleday, 1959), p. 100.

9. *JD* 7:63.

10. *JD* 7:163.

11. *JD* 18:215.

12. *JD* 16:151.

13. Though almost always indifferent, in short-lived episodes Laman and Lemuel had their hearts softened; it was real but did not last (see 1 Nephi 17:52–55). Real faith, like real humility, is developed "because of the word," which proves constant, and not because of surrounding circumstances, which change (see Alma 32:13–14).

14. See *Teachings,* p. 59.

15. *JD* 2:267.

16. *Lectures on Faith* 3:5.

17. See Stanley Weintraub, *Long Day's Journey into War* (New York: Truman Talley Books/Plume, 1992), pp. 214, 253.

18. *JD* 9:292.

Scripture Index

OLD TESTAMENT

NEW TESTAMENT

BOOK OF MORMON

11:43	103	3 Nephi	
12:15	54, 75	11:11	20
13:3	51, 69	12:48	44
17:5	14	18:24	20
26:27	14	21:9	56
29:3	115	21:10	96
30:13, 15	46	26:9–11	70
30:17	27	27:27	20, 29, 44,
31:5	97		47
32	106	28:1	25
32:13–14	128		
32:28	41	Mormon	
32:28–29	105	2:18	57
32:34	89	5:11	47
34:5	10	6:17	47
34:10	42	8:5	58
34:12	25	9:32, 34	61
34:15–17	97		
34:17	29	Ether	
37:8	103	12:6	12, 41
40:23	103	12:19	6
41:7	75	12:26–27	19, 115
41:10	95	12:27	35, 84
43:48	11	12:28–29	84
48:19	50	15:34	53
56:16	14		
		Moroni	
Helaman		7:28	40
3:29	47, 51	7:31–32	40
5:12	51	7:39, 41	41
12:3	101	8:26	109
16:15	123	9:20	103

DOCTRINE AND COVENANTS

1:14	95	3:12	64
1:20	4, 92	5:7	57, 61
1:21	4, 60	9:5–7	65
1:21–29	116	9:8	65
1:29	59	9:11	65
1:31	24	10:4	39, 59, 117

PEARL OF GREAT PRICE

Subject Index